Suffering For Spirit

Suffering For Spirit
Empowerment Through Ordeal

Thista Minai

Ellhorn Press
Hubbardston, Massachusetts

Ellhorn Press
12 Simonds Hill Road
Hubbardston, MA 01452

Suffering For Spirit: Empowerment Through Ordeal
© 2020 Thista Minai
ISBN 978-1-73450-320-3

Cover design by Catalina Castells, ©2020.
Find more information at CatalinaCastells.com.

All rights reserved. Unless otherwise specified,
no part of this book may be reproduced in any form
or by any means without the permission of the author.

Distributed in cooperation with
Lulu Enterprises, Inc.
860 Aviation Parkway, Suite 300
Morrisville, NC 27560

Contents

Acknowledgements... *i*
Content Warning.. *ii*
Introduction: Seeking the Spirit .... *iv*

Part I Understanding Ordeal
1: What Is Ordeal? 1
2: Terminology 11
3: Accepting Risk 19

Part II Sacred Crisis
4: Contemplating Change 25
5: Catharsis 27
6: Discovery... 33
7: Challenge 38
8: Relief... 43
9: Offering... 47

Part III Intentional Suffering
10: The Anatomy of Ordeal 53
11: Safer Seeking... 54
12: Determining Intent 59
13: Choosing the Method 66
14: Foundations for Communication 76
15: Planning Aftercare.. 88
16: Ritual Preparation 93
17: Approach 108
18: Crisis 113
19: Change 116
20: Recovery.. 120

Part IV Seeking Change
21: The Seeker's Role 125
22: Crafting Intent 126
23: Choosing a Facilitator 130
24: The Art of Becoming.. 136
25: Avoiding Ritual Dependence..................................... 142

Part V The Ordeal Path
26: Living Ordeal 147
27: Value in Suffering.. 149
28: Cultivating Resilience.. 154
29: Avoiding Expectation 158
30: Witnessing Change 160

Epilogue: The Fool's Journey.. 164
Appendix: Suggested Resources 166

Acknowledgements

From casual conversation to constructive criticism, more people have contributed to the making of this book than I can mention here. My thanks to all of you.

In particular, I must express gratitude and appreciation to:

Maureen, for my first catharsis.

Lemaris, for lighting my way.

Del, for opening the gate.

Wintersong, for sending me down the rabbit hole.

Xanthine, for teaching me about ordeal, and about myself.

Greg and Ay, for trusting me with the Temple.

Nelson and Imp, for your wisdom and friendship.

Raven, for all you taught me about ordeal and more, for all your hard work on this project, and for respecting my voice even when we don't agree.

Josh, for making these pages look as good as they do.

Cat, for saving the day with cover art.

Carter and Charles, for helping me pull through at the end.

Arkcane, for all your love, care, and support.

Finally, to every seeker I have ever worked with: Thank you. Yes, *you*. You might think I don't remember you, but I do. Your journey was for you, but I learned so much by watching you travel. Thank you for teaching me.

For even past suffering brings delight to one who has endured much, and wandered much.
–Homer, The Odyssey, Book 15, 400-401

Content Warning

This book is intended for adults. Ethically engaging in the practices presented here requires informed consent, and that informed consent requires emotional, mental, and social maturity in all participants.

This book touches on many subjects that people might find challenging, distressing, or even triggering. Topics include, but are not limited to, rape, bullying, grief, divorce, violence, ableism, racism, and other forms of systemic oppression.

All of these subjects are discussed in a context that emphasizes the importance of consent and agency for people who have undergone traumatic experiences, as well as explicit recognition that what is good or helpful for one person may do nothing or be hurtful to another. While I hope that I have navigated these topics well enough for this book to be accessible to most readers, no solution is universal, and compassionate discussion of a triggering subject can still trigger. Thus, I encourage you, dear reader, to make an informed choice about reading this book.

If you decide to continue, consider creating in your mind a brave space, wherein challenge undertaken by choice can lead to positive growth. Read as slowly as you need to. When something hits home in an uncomfortable way, stop and take a break. Take slow deep breaths, and notice how that air feels moving in and out of your body. You don't have to finish reading right away, or ever. Come back to it in a month, or a year, or leave it behind entirely. Make whatever choice is right for you.

Throughout this book, you will find sidebars explaining terminology or customs common in certain subcultures. The majority of my personal experience with ordeal has intertwined either with the BDSM subculture or the Neo-Pagan religious demographic. The sidebars are designed to inform readers who are not familiar with either or both of those demographics, and prevent confusion and misunderstanding.

Introduction: Seeking the Spirit

Hello, reader. Welcome to a little corner of my mind, wherein I apply the full force of language to ideas that buck the reins of articulation. I am attempting to present these concepts in a way that does not press or rely upon any particular spiritual or religious view. Nevertheless, I must disclose my views, as well as my background as it pertains to ordeal, because that background is the shape of my bias.

What I put forth here is what I have learned through experience. This book is intended for laypeople—others who, like me, have no professional background in psychology. I continually strive to educate myself on subjects relevant to ordeal, but that does not make me a mental health professional, nor do I attempt to operate as such. My experience came from Paganism, ritual, and kink. Explaining what all that means essentially mounts to telling a tiny slice of my life history; if you'd rather skip this and dive into the ordeal stuff, just read the last two paragraphs of this introduction, as my main point is there.

> Paganism, sometimes referred to as "Neo-Paganism" in order to differentiate it from indigenous spirituality, is a modern religion based on the religious practices of ancient Western civilizations and cultures. It is usually polytheistic or pantheistic. Wicca is the single largest sect, but there are many others sects which do not resemble Wicca.

At thirteen years old, I discovered that Tarot cards were a real thing, not an invention of movies or cartoons, and I set out to learn them. Unable to buy a deck of my own, I checked out a book on Tarot from the local library, and then copied the pictures in the book onto note cards. As I drew, I read about the images and what they were meant to symbolize. Certainly I did not understand back then everything I was reading and drawing, but I remembered those archetypes—the High Priestess and her intuitive secrets, Death as transformation, the falling Tower that precedes the Star of Hope, and the Fool who stands on the edge of a cliff as the journey begins. These seeds of the occult were planted in my mind, and would add color to my emerging spiritual self.

Three years later I discovered that Witchcraft too was a real religious practice. My father caught me reading books about Wicca, both eclectic and traditional. He confessed that he had also studied the occult when he was young, and assured me that this phase would pass. (Sorry, Dad.) Once I turned eighteen I joined a Wiccan coven, and began what ultimately amounted to fifteen years of formal training.

I was introduced to the concept of Ordeal through Raven Kaldera, a Pagan shaman and priest whom I met as I was still pursuing my first-degree initiation. As I got to know Raven, as well as the people he was training to lead conscious, intentional ordeal rituals, I saw sacred experiences that were nothing like what I'd been part of before. People were experiencing pain, but that pain transformed into power. I was curious right from the outset, and devoured Raven's book *Dark Moon Rising*, but I was not yet at the right place in my life to embrace ordeal.

What now seems like a lifetime later, and after a divorce that tested my understanding of who I was, I found myself at a Pagan gathering, participating in a ritual called "The Scourge and the Kiss". The title was a reference to a piece of liturgy from British Traditional Wicca, in which the Goddess of Life descends into the underworld to learn all Mysteries. There She meets the God of Death, and eventually receives both His scourge and His kiss. In the ritual inspired by this myth, participants chose to stand in one of two circles, their position indicating what role they would take and with whom they would interact. Each individual chose how clothed or unclothed they wanted to be, purely for their own comfort, as the ritual was nonsexual. People in the outer circle flogged people in the inner circle, while an officiator standing in the center guided

> "Flogging" is a term used in BDSM circles for a noninjurious whipping, usually on the upper back, buttocks, and possibly the chest (all muscle-padded areas) that can range in intensity from mild discomfort to some bruising, although rarely enough to break the skin and never enough to damage underlying structures. It is usually done with a "cat" or "flogger", an implement with multiple flat tails, usually of leather.

and monitored the ritual. People in the inner circle used hand gestures to communicate their experience of the flogging to the person flogging them, allowing for individual adjustment, and ensuring consensual participation. These unique personal experiences came together in a group energy raising that was powerfully transformative for all of us.

Immediately I knew I'd found something important. By then I'd come to feel that there was something missing in my spiritual path, and in that ritual I found it. I wanted to learn what that was, and how to create it. I wanted to learn ordeal. I approached Del Tashlin, the person who had designed the ritual, and asked if he would teach me. He agreed.

Del and I didn't live very close to one another, so the bulk of that education involved communicating what I had already learned about ritual through other training, and learning how to apply those skills to ordeal. Once we had a solid sense of where my knowledge needed to be filled in and patched up, we planned a weekend-long intensive to cover those points. At the end of that weekend, he gifted me with one of the floggers we'd used during practice, which remains to this day one of my most treasured tools. I asked Del what I needed to do next in order to continue my training, and he said I'd done all the training I could do; the next step was to facilitate an ordeal under the supervision of someone more experienced. Del referred me to Wintersong Tashlin, who was at the time responsible for the ordeal rituals at a major BDSM convention. With Del's recommendation, I was taken on as a co-facilitator.

Now, before this moment I had been aware of kink and BDSM as sexual practices. I'd even had an unexpectedly profound experience at a BDSM house party, which helped me recognize that the flogging ritual contained the missing piece I was seeking in my spiritual life. I had no idea, however, that there was a thriving kink *community*, and had no concept of what a kink convention would be like. (For definitions and explanations of the terms "BDSM" and "kink", please see *Chapter 1: What Is Ordeal?*)

I arrived at the convention venue completely focused on doing my job. I was there to facilitate an ordeal, so that's what I would do. I would not have sex, I would not do any scenes, and I would *certainly* not fall in love, because I was there to work. Of course, that is not how any of that turned out, except that I did my job at least well enough that I was brought back the next year as the lead facilitator.

Over the next several years I found myself drifting farther away from the Pagan community, and diving even deeper into the kink community. In Paganism the very idea of ordeal was (and perhaps still is) controversial, whereas in kink the concept is very familiar, even if the words we use to talk about it can vary tremendously. Kink also championed the value of authenticity, which is at the core of my spiritual beliefs, and taught me the value of a broad approach to spirituality. I learned how teaching fundamental concepts can encourage people to apply those concepts in whatever ways are right for them, and how this approach conveys respect for the uniqueness of each individual.

While I now feel a greater sense of home in the kink community than in the Pagan community, that certainly does not mean that I am no longer religious, or that ordeal is not a spiritual practice for me. Ordeal is fundamentally sacred to me because it helps people acknowledge, embrace, and become themselves. This is, in my mind, a sacred act, and to help someone accomplish it is sacred work.

Sometimes specific ordeal rituals are also sacred to me in a more explicitly religious way, most obviously when they are performed with or for specific deities. I will periodically share snapshots of my spiritual experiences in this book, but consider these solely as my personal examples. Do not measure your experiences against mine, and know that I value human diversity. Not only do I believe we are not all the same, I believe we *shouldn't* all be the same. I will also include examples from other people, many of whom do not share my religious or spiritual views. Consider the samples I present, and make up your own mind about what you want ordeal to mean to you.

All that said, one area in which I am utterly unapologetic about my bias is consent. My approach carries a tremendous emphasis on the importance of consent for all participants in any activity. Part of this approach is a result of my personal beliefs, but also everything I have learned from psychology suggests that a consent-heavy approach to ordeal offers the best potential outcomes for everyone involved. Furthermore, suffering inflicted without consent is abuse.

While I worked on this book, colleagues from both the Pagan and BDSM communities asked me, "Who are you writing this for? Who is your audience?" Certainly it is important to know your audience as you write, but the question always left me feeling uncomfortable. I didn't like the implication that this book could only be for certain people. I wanted it to be for everyone, so I attempted to use widely comprehensible language, and explain any subculture-specific terms and concepts.

Whether you are devoutly religious, staunchly atheist, or anything in between, the "spirit" of suffering matters in ordeal, but that "spirit" doesn't have to be about Gods or energy or animism or anything else, unless that type of connection is meaningful to you. What it *does* have to be about is *you*. The spirit you're suffering for is the spirit of who you are, the fundamental essence behind descriptions and declarations. Ordeal challenges our preconceptions about ourselves, and reveals our hidden strengths. To undergo an ordeal is to dare to see what you have been hiding in your shadows, to embrace the spirit of your self, and to remake the person you present to the world in accordance with your identity and your will.

Part I
Understanding Ordeal

Chapter 1: What Is Ordeal?

Today there are many different definitions of and approaches to "ordeal" working their way into the modern vernacular. The word "ordeal" comes from Proto-Germanic roots meaning "judgment" or "that which is dealt out". Historically an ordeal was a severe physical test which could prove a person's guilt or innocence. Now the word has become a sort of umbrella term for many types of transformational and often sacred work, including certain traditions of indigenous peoples, as well as some experiences in "modern primitive" groups. This book focuses on experiences that are indeed severe, extreme, and testing, but they are not necessarily about determining guilt or innocence, nor are they necessarily derived from indigenous practices.

> The term "modern primitive" was coined by the late educator and performer Fakir Musafar to describe modern adaptations of tribal practices such as tattooing, piercing, and other body modification practices inspired by the transition rites of indigenous cultures. (Check the appendix for further reading.)

The word "ordeal" still has no single commonly accepted definition. I will propose a definition shortly, but please understand that I do not believe this to be the "only" or "correct" definition. Rather, it is a way of articulating ordeal work that I find useful because it helps both me and those with whom I work understand what we are seeking, and how we need to go about that search.

The ordeals we shall examine in this book use an intentional engagement with suffering to reveal the innermost essence of our true selves, empower us to embrace who we really are, and challenge us to become who we want to be. These ordeals can be deliberately sought in ritual, but they can also be stumbled upon accidentally, or thrust upon us by life itself. That said, life is full of suffering, and just because an experience is painful or difficult doesn't necessarily mean it's an ordeal.

To understand the definition of ordeal in this book, we must first examine certain other concepts with which it overlaps and intersects. The world of kink in particular harbors a thriving community of ordeal workers, with about as many different definitions of "ordeal" as there are practitioners.

The word "kink" is typically used to describe unusual or unconventional sexual inclinations, ideas, and practices. It is arguably an umbrella term under which BDSM exists, although many people use the two expressions interchangeably, and still others claim that the two are quite different. BDSM is an acronym referring to commonly paired concepts: bondage and discipline, domination and submission, and sadism and masochism. Here we see an emphasis on activities that are not necessarily sexual, and indeed the history of BDSM includes a stark division between kink and sex, which has now begun to shift towards sex-positivity in some regions. Thus, kink and BDSM today can be thought to include activities which are unconventional, delightful to the practitioner, and sometimes but not always sexual in nature.

Ordeal has found a home in the kink community because kinky people are already accustomed to the idea that an action which one person might regard as unpleasant—being spanked, for example—could be desirable to another. This fundamental agreement on the subjective nature of experience allows "kinksters" to build a community in which it is acceptable and even expected that different people performing the same action can get different internal (and sometimes even external) results. Thus, a person having an experience of empowerment or transformation emerging from struggle is not too difficult to understand within the context of kink, where one person's pain is another's pleasure.

Many practitioners view ordeal as a spiritual discipline. I myself believe that anything which helps a person embrace their true selves and become who they

> Practitioners of BDSM have developed a wide range of tools and techniques that create intense and potentially quite painful physical sensations with carefully mitigated risks. BDSM practitioners negotiate physical and emotional concerns prior to beginning a "scene" or interaction, then adjust how they go about each activity to fall within their predetermined parameters.

want to be is inherently sacred. Nevertheless, I prefer to take an ecumenical approach to ordeal work. While I might view that process as sacred, some people won't; I see no conflict here. People of any spiritual or religious belief, or of none at all, can seek profound change and empowerment through ordeal experiences. We must each work in our own way, with the beliefs and practices that are right for each of us. For some that will include a measure of spirituality, religion, or sacredness. For others it will not.

Pain, struggle, and anguish come in many forms, but they do not always elicit change and empowerment. Similarly, many types of kink, BDSM, ritual, and spiritual practice can be empowering and transformational, but they are not all ordeals as I would define them. To be quite clear, I do not believe that non-ordeal experiences are in any way less important or less sacred than ordeal experiences. They simply function through different mechanics. As you can read shortly, I choose to define "ordeal" somewhat narrowly because it allows us to consider more clearly what factors contribute to a constructive experience, and how we can avoid unintentional trauma.

What, then, makes an ordeal what it is?

Whether it be an intentionally designed experience, or a struggle encountered by chance, four core factors come together to create an ordeal:

Suffering

Suffering does not always mean physical pain. While there are certainly both physiological and psychological reasons that physical pain is so frequently used as a tool for transformation in ordeal, mental and emotional suffering can sometimes be more challenging than bodily pain. The point of suffering in ordeal is not to reach some predetermined threshold for physical discomfort. The goal is to challenge some element of who we are, and either strengthen that piece of ourselves by enduring difficulty, or tear it from ourselves if we discover that it is not what we want or need to be. In order to test our sense of self in this way, ordeals must be difficult. Without suffering, there is no challenge, and thus no ordeal.

Consider physical healing as a metaphor: Sometimes ordeal is like physical therapy. We must stretch parts of ourselves that are scarred from injury, strengthen parts that are atrophied from lack of use, or learn how to inhabit a body that is healing from trauma. Stretching hurts, and exercising burns, but it's a good hurt, and a healthy burn, and without them we are not pushing ourselves hard enough to get better. Of course, stretching too aggressively or overworking a muscle can cause further injury, and this too is true of ordeal. The suffering we seek is enough to challenge us, to push us to reevaluate ourselves and claim who we are, but not so extreme that it damages us. Finding that line between healthy challenge and destructive hardship can be one of the most difficult and perilous elements of ordeal by design. Finding a way to see life's challenges as constructive ordeals—particularly when there is just nothing good about a situation—is what makes walking the ordeal path as a way of life so arduous.

Sometimes ordeal is like surgery. When some part of who we are is simply no longer healthy, we must cut into ourselves and repair or remove the piece that holds us back. Just as surgery must take place in a sterile setting to avoid infection, and be practiced by a qualified surgeon to avoid complications, ordeals require a carefully prepared environment and a skilled facilitator to avoid causing more damage than they heal. And just as even the best surgeon in the world cannot guarantee a 100% success rate, no ordeal is entirely without risk.

The Mindset of the Seeker

Suffering alone does not make an ordeal, any more than being cut with a scalpel always counts as surgery. The mindset of the person suffering determines how they process and internalize that experience. Consequently, the mindset of the seeker—the person undergoing the experience—is the most important factor in any ordeal. The primary job of a person facilitating an ordeal is to help the seeker achieve a mindset conducive to their intent.

There is no point at which enough pain or enough suffering will automatically cause an experience to become an ordeal. A stubbed toe is not something one would generally think of as an ordeal, and creating an ordeal out of a hurt toe is not simply a matter of ramping up the pain. Theoretically, you could smash someone's toe with a hammer, and still end up with a dissatisfied seeker who has a broken toe. On the other hand, if you help a seeker understand a long walk along a difficult trail as a metaphor for traversing a difficult period in their life, a stubbed toe contextualized in the right way can be just enough of a catalyst to open up a new understanding of who they are, where they are, and why they're there.

As I began to study ordeal ritual, some of those I learned from believed that a facilitator must be ready to push a seeker past the point when they try to end a ritual if they have not yet reached epiphany, and that seekers should only engage in an ordeal with a facilitator they can trust in this way. In the world of kink and BDSM, this would equate to continuing a scene past the point where one person uses their safeword to end an encounter. (To learn more about safewords, see *Chapter 14: Foundations for Communication*.) As I have matured as an individual and as a facilitator, I have come to disagree strongly with this sentiment.

To begin with, consent is the foundation of our ethical justification not only for ordeal work, but for kink and BDSM as well. If we as travelers on the ordeal path begin to weaken that foundation, we hurt everyone. Activists fighting for the rights of kinksters everywhere depend on the fundamental concept that we are all consenting adults, that we are aware of what we are doing, informed of the risks we take, and do what we do willingly. When we obfuscate consent in our ordeals, we make the work of those activists more difficult, and we give those unsavory few who would circumvent or undermine consent a gray area in which to disguise their assault.

Consent is not a thing handed over in a transaction between seeker and facilitator. It is a state that must be achieved and maintained by all participants. A seeker may well consent to being pushed beyond their limits during initial negotiation, but that can change at any moment. We must allow ourselves ways to communicate, hear, and respond to those changes, even when someone actively wants their limits put to the test.

Furthermore, pushing someone past the point at which they have chosen to stop is much more likely to do harm than to help. When a seeker wants to abort an ordeal, their willingness to change has come to an end. They are much less likely to process or internalize their experience in a positive way. Perhaps they are not yet ready to face what stands in the way of the change they set out to make. Perhaps they have discovered that what they wanted is not what they need, and they must reconsider their path. Perhaps the entire point of their ordeal was learning that they *can* say no, that they can set limits and enforce them. Either way, no good will come of ignoring their request to stop, and someone who pushes forward anyway is no longer facilitating ordeal; they are committing assault.

We cannot force a seeker to change, even if that seeker is ourselves. A facilitator can and must carefully craft an environment that is most likely to produce constructive change, but, ultimately, the seeker must be willing to accept what they find in that space, and reshape themselves in light of what they encounter. Similarly, walking the ordeal path ourselves requires that we seek willingness, and remain open to what our suffering can teach us, even when we despise the suffering itself.

The Unknown or Inarticulable

In order for an ordeal to truly challenge us, it must contain some element of the unknown. Ordeal is a mirror that lets us see who we are. If we already knew what we'd see there, we wouldn't need to look. The entire point of ordeal is to help us face those corners of ourselves that we neglect, suppress, or hide from. When we already know who we are, and who we want to be, and how we must change to become ourselves, we can embrace the change we want. To be sure, that is a difficult process with its own elements of suffering, but it is a known suffering. We often suffer for things we understand and value. Ordeal means suffering to *gain* understanding.

Ordeals may also contain some element of inarticulable revelation, a moment of understanding so profound that no words can adequately describe it. For example, a ritual intended to create emotional catharsis, relieving the seeker's sense of guilt over wanting to leave her husband, instead became an ordeal of discovery when she realized that the facilitator could not hit her hard enough to make her cry, that her husband could not hurt her badly enough to force her to leave, that she could endure anything if she decided to do so, and the only way to escape her unhappy marriage was for her to choose to leave. Put into words, the revelation seems obvious, and had someone said as much to the seeker before her ordeal, she might have agreed on an intellectual level, but she did not understand that she had reached the point of needing to make that choice until suffering brought her clarity. By her own account of the experience, no description, no matter how articulate, could fully portray the profundity of that moment, and nothing but an ordeal could have brought her there.

Choosing ordeal means accepting that there is some piece of understanding we need that can only be found in the inarticulable moment of epiphany, that we can and must learn something in a moment of crisis. We must accept the unknown before we can learn. We cannot begin traveling to a place if we are already there.

Intent Without Expectation

Intent is essential in ordeal, for the facilitator tends the mindset of the seeker by accepting their intent and using it to guide them both through the experience. Expectation, however, sets us up to judge our experiences based on an artificial rubric, and primes the seeker for failure.

As discussed above, an effective ordeal must include some level of uncertainty for the seeker. This uncertainty could be as simple as the seeker facing a challenge without knowing if they will succeed or fail: they might know the details of the test they will face, but don't really know what it will be like to face it, or whether or not they will pass. All elements up until that challenge are predetermined, but past that point, all is unknown, and there must be no expectation of result, only acceptance of whatever happens.

Sometimes the seeker does not know anything at all about what an ordeal will entail until it begins. The seeker and facilitator discuss the intent of the experience, negotiate what types of challenges the seeker is willing to face, and then the facilitator creates a ritual within those parameters without the seeker knowing any of the details ahead of time. This forces the seeker to be present in the moment as the ritual happens, fully immersed in each second of the experience.

When we know the outline of a ritual or the details of an ordeal ahead of time, we cannot help having a preconceived notion of what it will be like. Experiencing the moment without weighing it against that expectation will be extremely difficult, and sometimes even impossible. This same concept of avoiding expectation is present in "mystery traditions" such as the ancient rites of Eleusis, or initiations in certain forms of contemporary Witchcraft. The rituals themselves are kept secret so that seekers may experience them without preconception. This lack of assumption allows them to accept unexpected revelations that might have been missed had they been preoccupied with attaining a specific result. When we abandon all foreknowledge of events to come, we have no choice but to take each experience as it is, for we have no preconceived notions to weigh them against.

Ordeals come in many different forms, both ritualized and otherwise, and in some of those cases we do know in an external sort of way what will happen—who will do or say what, or what we will have to do ourselves. Even in ordeals such as these, however, there is a point past which we have no prior knowledge, no way of knowing what that thing will be like, or what it will mean to experience it. Embracing this unknown without expectation of its affect or result allows us to find those pieces of ourselves that we sometimes didn't even know we needed to see.

A definition of the word "ordeal" determined by the presence of each of the core factors described above will seem limiting to some. There are many other types of powerful, sacred, and transformational experiences currently described by many as "ordeals" which would not quite fit into my definition. When speaking about ordeal with other ritual officiators and facilitators, I found the term to be used so broadly that clarification was inevitably necessary for discourse of any depth. These moments of needing to express myself more clearly are what led me to ask myself: what do I mean when I say "ordeal"? Why do I use that word, and to what purpose?

The definition offered above was the result of that years-long process of internal questioning, and my answer was doubtlessly colored by my frequent role as a facilitator. When I asked myself what "ordeal" means, I was also asking myself what I was about to do, and what my responsibilities were to the other person. This is why I find the concept of the four core factors so useful: it helps me both understand and express what I can offer as a facilitator, and what a seeker must put forth themselves.

Few people would disagree that suffering and mindset are integral to an ordeal experience, but the necessity of uncertainty and intent without expectation are often debated. These two elements are incredibly important to my definition of ordeal because they change the nature of an experience. Whether you call it an ordeal or not, a ritual with all four of my core factors is tremendously different from a ritual missing any single one of them; the very function of how and why they transform the seeker is fundamentally different.

Furthermore, creating a ritual with intentional uncertainty and without expectation require a special set of skills from a facilitator. One must be able to assist the seeker by both guiding and following at once, letting them show you where their suffering leads them, and showing them that they can dare to seek it. One must be ready to shift an experience or change a plan at a moment's notice when the unexpected requires something different, and one must be ready to apply the mental, emotional, and perhaps even spiritual equivalent of first aid in the event that something goes wrong. I define ordeal as I do partly to highlight the necessity of these skills in a facilitator, and partly to better articulate the unique intrapersonal utility of ordeal experiences.

In modern western occultism, polarity, synergy, and resonance are energy dynamics considered essential to raising mystical power. Discussions about esoteric ritual and mystic experience often involve some exploration of these dynamics and how they might apply in practice. After one such discussion, I found myself wondering why no one ever talks about dissonance as an energy dynamic. I asked myself what the power of dissonance might be, how it could be used and what it would be good for, and quickly realized that dissonance is the dynamic at work in ordeal.

Ordeal is the way we face things we can't face in any other way. We can't know how an ordeal is going to turn out because if we did it wouldn't be an ordeal, and this is the beauty and utility of ordeal work—

whatever the problem is, we can't just logically introspect and work out the thing, because it's unknowable and inarticulable. We can, however, have an indescribable feeling that something is there, an ambiguous sense that some blockage, or some shadow, or some *something* within us needs facing.

That knowing, that dread and need and fear and desire all rolled up into one, that compelling combination of attraction and aversion to some festering piece of ourselves ... that is the dissonance of ordeal. Ordeal work is the process of seeking that dissonance, of hearing those notes and listening to our souls and finding out why we're making that music. And just like in music, from there we either resolve the dissonance and become a new iteration of ourselves, or we learn how those dissonant notes fit into the greater symphony of our souls, and in context of the whole, the dissonance becomes concordant.

Whether through physical pain, emotional distress, spiritual anguish, or mental conflict, ordeals bring us to a state of challenge which tests our understanding of our own selves. Ordeals unlock possibilities we would never consider in comfort, and even just seeing those possibilities as viable options changes us—it changes our understanding of who we are, where we are, and where we are going. That intangible insight can be gained in no other way, for its meaning derives from its context. Once a seeker sets their foot upon the stage of ordeal, they *will* change, even if no one knows how the play will end.

Chapter 2: Terminology

Before proceeding any further, we must take some time to more fully investigate relevant terminology as it appears in this book. For all that I wish words were unequivocally literal and universal in meaning, they are not. Therefore, let me be clear about which words I use to describe what in this book, and why I chose those particular terms.

Seeker

I have already explained that the seeker is the person undergoing the ordeal, the individual who is to suffer and be challenged in some way. I use the term *seeker* because ordeals set us on a journey to find our own power. In ordeals we seek ourselves, and the more of us we find, the stronger we become.

In kink and BDSM, people often talk about the "top" or the "bottom" in a scene. In this paradigm, the "top" does things to the "bottom" - the "top" is the doer, and the "bottom" is the receiver. It is easy to assume that ordeal seekers are the bottoms of their experience, but this is not always true. Often the seeker has things done to them during an ordeal; for example, they might be bound to face fears of losing control, or be beaten to explore their own capacity for endurance. Sometimes, however, the seeker is the person doing things to someone else; a person raised to be too accommodating might suffer through screaming their true thoughts at a facilitator in order to learn that they too deserve to be heard, or a person philosophically dedicated to living in peace might need to hurt someone in order to confront their own secret craving for violence.

Some people prefer the term "ordeal dancer" instead of seeker, and certainly that title has a poetic appeal. One might argue that "ordeal dancer" better fits those moments when ordeals are not carefully crafted rituals, but rather experiences thrust upon us by life itself. However, even in these moments, as we shall discuss later, one's capacity to transform misery into empowerment rests in no small part on their willingness to change; in other words, the individual must *seek* their power.

Facilitator

An ordeal facilitator is an individual who designs, creates, or officiates ordeals for a seeker. In 2009, Raven Kaldera wrote the book *Dark Moon Rising*, which provides a fascinating and invaluable perspective on ordeal work. In this book, Kaldera uses the term Ordeal Master for what I call a facilitator.

Kaldera elaborates at great length about the duties and responsibilities of an Ordeal Master, stressing a necessity for both competence and humility, and affirming that the focus of the ordeal must be the seeker, not the facilitator. While I agree with the meaning and intent Kaldera puts forth in his definition, the term itself does not feel right to me. The word "Master" conveys power and ownership, nearly the opposite of humbly guiding someone through an experience meant to empower them. Kaldera takes care to clarify that "Master" is not meant in the context of a master and slave, but as in one who has mastered a skill. Even so, I am personally uncomfortable with the idea that I might have mastered the art of ordeal, since it is by its very definition filled with the unknowable, inarticulable, and intangible.

I prefer the title "facilitator", because it keeps emphasis where it belongs: on the seeker. The seeker must become the master of their own ordeal, for it is through mastery of some piece of themselves that they transform and gain personal power. Any individual curating that experience for them is facilitating change, not creating it. Certainly skilled facilitators will create more effective ordeals, and unskilled facilitators can do real damage, but ultimately the power rests in the seeker. In this sense, ordeal can be likened to chemistry: the seeker is a reaction wanting to happen. Some reactions won't happen at all without a catalyst to instigate change. Add the right catalyst, and the reaction can be more efficient, or more complete. Add the wrong catalyst, and the entire laboratory could explode.

Words have power. Kaldera and many others I've met who use the title "Ordeal Master" do so with humility and care. It is their semantics with which I am uncomfortable, not their intent. *Dark Moon Rising* is an excellent resource for students of ordeal, and Kaldera's skill and knowledge of ordeal facilitation are worthy of respect. I myself have sought his tutelage on multiple occasions. Nevertheless, I feel it is important to remember that our words will carry meaning to others who do not know what those terms mean to us, and we must be conscientious of the connotations—intentional or otherwise—present in our language.

Words also carry power in our own minds. This can be a valuable tool for affirmation and empowerment, but fancy titles can also give an inflated ego corners to hide in while it colors our judgment. I do not consider myself a master of ordeal, because to me personally that implies a connotation of having power over the art, or the ability to force a seeker into change they do not want, neither of which is true. I like having a title that keeps me humble, and reminds me of my limitations.

As a facilitator, I have mastered nothing. I am an imperfect being striving to help others in unconventional ways, and I can and will make mistakes. When I call myself a Master, I can forget my fallibility, and make it too easy to think I know enough already, that I have enough skill and experience, that I don't need to continue pushing myself to learn more. I don't feel that I can truly master ordeal because there is no limit to what I can learn, and no point at which failure is impossible.

Witness

The term witness requires no special definition, but the role of witnesses in ordeal work is worth some consideration. Witnesses are a common feature in many of our modern rites of passage. Weddings, funerals, and graduation ceremonies are just a few examples of contemporary rituals where witnesses play an important role. Often when we experience or accomplish change, we want others to see it, to know what we have done, and to make note of it. The word witness describes someone who has not only seen a thing, but who can provide evidence that it happened through their testimony. Witnesses help us document our experiences, and that documentation affirms our emerging sense of self.

Many seekers will want or even need witnesses present at their ordeals. These witnesses will need to be able to stay present in the seeker's experience, even when they are not actively involved in it. A facilitator curating an ordeal that includes witnesses will need to ensure that the witnesses remain engaged in a way that appropriately enhances the seeker's experience.

Just as some couples choose to elope, focusing their attention entirely on each other and their shared experience, some seekers may want to be alone in their suffering, with only a facilitator to guide them. Some trials need to be private, and sometimes the experience is an ordeal precisely *because* it is private. An individual accustomed to suffering for the attention of others may need to face what it is to suffer when no one can see it. Then again, the opposite can also be true. An individual accustomed to suffering alone may find that the true ordeal is letting someone else see their pain.

The presence or absence of witnesses can change the nature of an ordeal experience. Even in our unexpected life lesson ordeals, whether others acknowledge our suffering or not can change how we internalize our experience. By seeking or avoiding the attestation of others, we can engage with the concept of the witness as a tool for intentional change and empowerment.

Supporter

Supporters straddle the gray area between facilitators, who actively work to create ordeal experiences, and witnesses, who quietly hold space for those experiences. Supporters provide what is typically referred to in the BDSM demographic as "aftercare": time, attention, and resources for the purpose of recuperation after a challenging experience. The type of aftercare provided varies widely depending on the needs of the individuals receiving it. At the very least, it will be checking on a seeker's physical needs, and providing blankets, food, drink, etc. For some people it might mean offering a comforting embrace, shoulder to cry on, or an ear to listen. Others might ask that their supporter simply guard a space for them so that they can take a moment alone, without interruption, to enjoy peace and quiet, or process their experiences on their own.

While supporters can technically be considered a type of assistant facilitator, giving this particular role its own name helps us to recognize the unique function of supporters. Since anyone involved in an ordeal—whether it be a facilitator, a seeker, or even a witness—may need aftercare when the ritual is over, supporters are often not present at the ritual itself, ensuring that they are mentally, emotionally, and physical prepared to give support when it is needed. Some seekers may still need to receive some kind of aftercare from their facilitator, particularly when recognition or appreciation are key elements of the experience. In these cases, however, the seeker may still want some extra time when everything is done to reflect on their experience with a supporter, and the facilitator should definitely seek support for their own needs. (For more information, see *Chapter 15: Planning Aftercare.*)

Ordeal Work and Ordeal Ritual

Ordeal can arise in many different environments, from carefully orchestrated ritual experiences to unintentional side effects of intense encounters to completely unexpected moments of agonizing epiphany. Like so many others, I began my study of ordeal using the term rather broadly, and did not take care to semantically separate these different modes of engagement.

Then one day I met a woman and her partner at a weekend gathering for kink enthusiasts, and together we had a fascinating conversation about ordeal. The woman and I got along particularly well, and eventually we negotiated a scene in which energetic connection and shared presence were the ultimate goal. She mentioned that this might turn out to be an ordeal experience for her, which we both agreed to work with should it happen, but that was not what I was aiming for as we played together. The skills and techniques I brought to bear were aimed at connection, not ordeal.

The woman did in fact have an ordeal experience during our scene, but this was not at all a problem, as we had both consented to this possibility beforehand. Later on, however, I heard her describing our scene as an ordeal in a context which made it entirely unclear that this was not an intentional ordeal ritual. I did not appreciate her speaking publicly about the scene we had done as if I'd been acting as her ordeal facilitator, as these are very different modes of being for me. She didn't know this, having never worked with me as a facilitator, but, nevertheless, I felt misrepresented.

Always the ordeal enthusiast, I leaned into my discomfort, and had a constructive conversation with the woman about what happened and how we were talking about it. I did not want to discard or devalue her experience of the scene as an ordeal, but at the same time felt a strong need to communicate that I was not acting as an ordeal facilitator in that moment. What we agreed upon by the end of our conversation was a need for better language surrounding the many ways in which ordeal takes shape in our lives.

Since then I have taken care to describe "ordeal ritual" as a specific type of ordeal experience, and "ordeal work" is now the phrase I use when I want to inclusively describe all types of ordeal; any experience that features all of the four core factors is arguably an ordeal, and can fit under the "ordeal work" umbrella.

An **ordeal ritual** is an intentionally curated experience in which one or more facilitators carefully crafts an ordeal specifically designed to address the intent of one or more seekers. In an ordeal ritual, the seeker and facilitator agree upon an intent at the outset. Declaring this intent allows the facilitator to create a structured environment in which the seeker can confront what challenges them. This structure will not necessarily feel rigid or formal, but the facilitator will have at the very least a general sense of where they are going and how they plan to get there. Because of this structure, an ordeal ritual offers a much greater capacity to mitigate risk than unintended ordeal work encountered by chance. The facilitator will have at least some idea of what metaphorical buttons will be pushed in the seeker's mind and heart, and will have a very clear idea of what physical challenges await. Consequently, a facilitator of an ordeal ritual is responsible for taking appropriate steps to ensure that any planned activities will not cause unintentional harm, and must ensure that, should an ordeal go awry, appropriate urgent care and support is ready and available.

This level of preparation is impossible for unexpected ordeal work, which is by definition unplanned. All negotiation for any type of play, be it kinky fun or an intense challenge, should involve at least some plan for what to do in case things don't go as expected. Consider including in this contingency plan a negotiated course of action in the event of an ordeal experience. Ask each other what you would want to do, and what you would want to be responsible for.

In a typical kink scene where ordeal is not our goal, should the person I'm playing with begin to approach ordeal I will be ready to respond—either by adjusting what we're doing to avoid that inner challenge, or by offering them support as they embrace it, or by doing whatever else we agreed to in our negotiation ahead of time. I would not, however, intentionally lead them towards a point of conflict they want to face. They might still find and face that conflict, but I would not be facilitating their journey.

In an ordeal ritual, the person's intent to face that conflict would be explicitly stated from the outset, and I would intentionally work to guide them in that direction. My every action would be aimed at contextualizing that person's suffering so as to make it constructively relevant to their stated goal, and I will have created an environment that supports them in positively integrating whatever they learn in their moment of crisis.

While the outcome of these two experiences might be extremely similar, the actions and responsibilities of the people engaged in them are quite different. Creating more explicit language for different types of ordeal allows people to better understand what they want, not just from the experience itself but also from the people involved. One of the ways ordeal experiences go awry is when one person expects a certain amount of support or facilitating from the other and doesn't receive it, or when someone feels a person is demanding more of their time and care than was previously agreed on. Differentiating ordeal ritual from other ordeal experiences is one way to elucidate negotiations around who is responsible for what. Kink scenes should involve this level of communication and negotiation anyway, and the benefit of using specific terminology is that everyone will more clearly understand what is expected of them, and plan accordingly.

The Ordeal Path

Since embarking on my own journey on the ordeal path, I have contemplated many different definitions of that particular set of words. What makes the ordeal path a path? Does participating in an ordeal automatically make someone a traveler on that path, or is there more to that journey?

Raven Kaldera and Lee Harrington each write about the ordeal path as one avenue in a set of eight paths of power. The concept of the eightfold path, or eight paths of power, can arguably be traced to British Traditional Wicca, and was doubtless inspired or at least influenced by many other religious and magical systems. Kaldera and Harrington each define the eight paths slightly differently. Kaldera writes of them as categories of shamanic techniques, while Harrington describes them as tools for cultivating spiritual and sexual awareness. Both of these approaches put forth the ordeal path as an avenue to personal power, and in this sense I can agree. Ordeal is indeed a way in which we can seek our own strength. Nevertheless, I sought a broader interpretation of the ordeal path. I wanted a way to look at ordeal as a more comprehensive concept for engaging with the world. I sought a way of life.

The ordeal path, as I see it, is a way of living by embracing suffering as an opportunity for empowerment. To be sure, this is difficult, for life often thrusts unwanted adversity upon us. Some of those challenges might be seen later as "for the best" in the long run, but some are simply terrible, and no amount of perspective will make them "good". Walking the ordeal path is not a fancy term for optimism, nor an ignorant suggestion to solve all problems by seeking the silver lining of every situation. The ordeal path means accepting terrible things as terrible, and consciously choosing how we wish to navigate them. In the words of ordeal facilitator Asrik Tashlin, "We discover who we are in the difficult choices we make." To walk the ordeal path is to acknowledge suffering, fully feel our own anguish, and ask ourselves, "What does this show me about who I am?"

Chapter 3: Accepting Risk

Ordeal is full of risk. Should you choose to engage with ordeal in any capacity, you will best serve yourself and others by acknowledging the risks involved, and taking what steps you can to mitigate those risks.

To begin with, ordeals do not "fix" anything. An ordeal is more like a mirror than a cure; it shows you the parts of yourself you cannot see with your own eyes. Ordeals begin work, or help it along, but they almost never end it. Ordeal is a tool for seeking solutions; it is not the solution itself.

In an ideal world, everyone participating in ordeal work, be it as a facilitator, seeker, or even witness, would do so under the guidance of a qualified personal therapist. While ordeal is not therapy in the clinical sense, it is certainly therapeutic, and there is a real danger in letting someone with no background in psychology or psychiatry poke at the shadows of your psyche. Having a therapist to help you contextualize and process an ordeal experience can fundamentally change your outcome.

I am fortunate enough to have an excellent therapist with whom I can speak frankly on any subject. They help me maintain an awareness of my own baggage and biases, which makes me less likely to project those issues onto seekers who come to me for facilitation. They also help me recognize signs that might indicate neurodivergence in a seeker, which lets both the seeker and I more accurately assess whether or not I have the necessary skill to facilitate for them within each of our definitions of acceptable risk.

> *Neurodivergence*, as a term, was coined by the neurodivergent activist Kassiane Asasumasu, and refers to individuals whose neurology departs from the standard norm in a way that has a marked effect on their life experience; e.g. autism, ADD, epilepsy, traumatic brain injury, Tourette Syndrome, etc.

To be clear, my therapist cannot diagnose someone they have never met. They are not a foolproof way of detecting anything. When they point out an item worthy of concern, both they and I are acutely aware that it is an observation based on secondhand information, not an indisputable fact. Those observations prompt further discussion between myself and the seeker, and the seeker and I determine how to proceed from there.

Similarly, just because my therapist helps me cultivate awareness of my own biases does not mean I will never subject someone else to them. While I can certainly strive not to project my mental and emotional baggage on a seeker, my way of thinking is part of my bias. In that sense, the best I can offer is to be as forthright as possible about what my bias is, and let seekers choose willingly to engage with my internal filter.

In an ideal world, all participants in ordeal will have a therapist available to help them process their experiences in a way that is healthy for them ... but our world is not ideal. Mental health services are woefully difficult to attain in the United States of America. This difficulty is compounded for people who are part of any minority, or who engage in unconventional practices such as BDSM. It is tough for an average heterosexual white cisgendered man to find an appropriate and affordable therapist. For a kinky Pagan trans-person of color, it can be immeasurably difficult. Even people who can find compatible therapists often can't afford them. Some therapists accept health insurance, but many don't, and some people don't have health insurance (it is my deepest hope that this changes in the future, but at the time of this writing, universal healthcare is still not a reality in the United States of America).

To require that everyone engaging in ordeal work also seek licensed therapy ignores the reality that therapy is not equally accessible to all. We might all wish for it, but it is not universally available, and what is available is not always helpful. Telling people to "just get therapy" only reinforces privilege and the prejudices that go along with it. We can and should speak frankly about the benefits of therapy, encouraging its use and decreasing stigma around the idea of "seeing a shrink", but we must also accept that therapy will not always be accessible, and be ready to proceed with caution and care.

Many people have asked me over the years why I would teach about something that is so dangerous. Don't I worry that someone who attends one of my ordeal classes or reads my writing will attempt more than they can handle and do real harm?

Yes, I do worry, but I will teach anyway. People will do ordeals whether I write about them or not. People are already doing them, and have been doing them far longer than I have been alive. My arrival on the scene did not create ordeal work, and my silence will not stop it. What I *can* do is educate people to the best of my ability about what they are doing. I can share what I have learned, as others shared with me, and help people make informed choices about the risks they take.

I suspect that this book is unlikely to introduce someone to ordeal work as an entirely new concept. I am guessing that you, dear reader, had some sense of ordeal before you began reading; that even if you had never heard the term "ordeal" before, or never used it in this way, you recognize what I am describing at least in part from some other area of your life. The purpose of this book is not to create something new, but to help people better understand and communicate with one another on a subject that is as old as humanity itself.

Intentionally pursuing ordeal work comes with a burden of responsibility. Awareness forfeits the luxury of ignorance. Whether you are a facilitator, a seeker, a witness, or a supporter, you must acknowledge the risks of what you are attempting. Psychological and physical risks shall be discussed further in *Chapter 11: Safer Seeking* and *Chapter 13: Choosing the Method* respectively, but these are not the only risks to consider. Learn what legal restrictions apply where you live, and make sure all parties involved are aware of those laws when you decide what activities you will consent to. Keep in mind that even if an ordeal ritual goes perfectly for everyone involved, an unexpected spectator can do real harm by misrepresenting your ritual to an unsympathetic public.

Frantically taking steps to protect your reputation, however, is not the solution here. The solution is mutually informed risk-aware consent, and the only way to get there is through genuinely attempted clear communication conducted in good faith by all participants. *Chapter 11: Safer Seeking*, *Chapter 13: Choosing the Method*, and *Chapter 14: Foundations for Communication* will explore how to go about that in more depth, but for now keep this in mind: when we communicate, negotiate, and plan with the intent to protect our reputations, we have already failed. Defensiveness can deafen us, and we must be able to hear the people we are working with in order to understand their limits and desires. We must communicate, negotiate, and plan with the goal of constructive transformation for the seeker at the root of everything we say, every choice we make, and every risk we take.

Nothing can remove all the risks in ordeal. This work is immeasurably powerful, and immensely dangerous. Whether you wish to engage as a witness, supporter, seeker, or facilitator, you must acknowledge that danger, and then, with full awareness, choose to move through it.

Part II
Sacred Crisis

Chapter 4: Contemplating Change

Ordeal can be a powerful tool for transformation: a moment of crisis breaks apart an old way of being, and a new dimension of self, awakened in agony, reveals strength and depth of awareness that the seeker could not have imagined before. Such broad concepts, however, are difficult to grasp in a practically meaningfully way. We know we are talking about engaging with difficult things in order to elicit change, but what types of difficult things, and what kinds of change?

One useful way to conceptualize ordeal work is to categorize the types of experiences a seeker might have. The categories we shall explore are catharsis, relief, discovery, challenge, and offering. Dividing the subject of ordeal in this way makes discussion easier, and allows us to dig into the biological and psychological mechanics of these different experiences.

Nevertheless, this attempt at categorization leaves us with two conceptual problems. First, due to the ultimately unknowable nature of the ordeal, a seeker often doesn't know what type of experience they need until they are having it. Our categories are useful for helping us explore what types of change and empowerment one can achieve in ordeal work, but designing an ordeal experience must be handled differently. For this reason, the art of intentionally designing an ordeal experience will have its own section in this book.

We must also note that our ordeal types do not behave like discrete categories. They are more like attributes, each one affecting the nature of the experience. When describing an object, we generally use multiple attributes together to give the listener a better sense of the thing we're trying to convey. The thing is not just those attributes themselves, but the attributes are part of what makes that thing what it is. For example, a tennis ball is something more specific than just a round and bouncy object, but it wouldn't be a tennis ball if it weren't round, or bouncy, or both round and bouncy. Ordeals too generally involve multiple attributes, each one interacting with the others to create a unique and specific experience.

Understanding ordeal work can be approached through examining these attributes in the same way that examining the physical properties of a sphere gives clues about what makes a good tennis ball. Each attribute provides an essential function, and we must be familiar with each of these functions separately before we can begin piecing them together into something more complex.

Chapter 5: Catharsis

Catharsis means cleansing, purification, or purgation. Today it generally refers to the release of and resulting relief from strong emotions. This usage comes from a metaphor made by Aristotle to explain how spectators of ancient Greek plays were emotionally purified and renewed as they watched dramatic tragedies.

Our modern culture in the United States of America generally frowns on the expression of strong emotions, especially sadness, anger, and other supposedly negative emotions. The culturally acquired inhibition against showing one's true feelings can be so strong that some people find it hard to scream or cry at all, even in private, no matter how angry or sad they are. For these individuals, cathartic ordeal can provide necessary release.

When we watch a sad movie and cry over the ending, or scream when a monster jumps at the screen in a horror film, we are given a culturally appropriate excuse to emote. While our emotions may not be sourced by our own experience, they provide real relief all the same. Ordeal catharsis functions on a similar premise. When someone needs to cry but can't, consensually hitting them until their body's physiological response results in tears can open floodgates to necessary expression. When someone needs to scream and yell and fight, giving them someone to fight back against can provide the outlet they need, or provoking them until their shell of composure cracks can provide a necessary relief.

In his book *Sacred Pain*, Ariel Glucklich explores the human body's physiological and psychological responses to physical pain. Three of his observations are particularly relevant to catharsis. To begin with, pain serves a biological purpose; it tells the brain that something is wrong, or that something requires attention and needs to change. Facilitators can use that physiological cue to incite emotional and psychological change in a seeker.

Pain also has the effect of quieting the mind. As Glucklich puts it, "An extreme bombardment of incoming signals, in whatever sensory modality, can produce a virtual shutdown of outgoing signals..." A flood of painful stimuli from a flogger, for example, can create a sense of clarity in the mind of a seeker, allowing them to let go of self destructive mental habits or emotional patterns, and make space for constructive change.

Finally, pain demands attention. Inflicting pain on a seeker while calling their attention to their purpose through dialogue brings their focus to the issue at hand, even despite strong subconscious desires to avoid it. Catharsis occurs when the seeker can no longer ignore the source of their suffering, and must choose to let it go, or choose to bear it and let go of their anguish over carrying it.

Catharsis is extremely common in the world of kink and BDSM. My own introduction to the world of ordeal came upon me unexpectedly during a flogging scene. As the woman hit me harder and harder, I began to cry, even though I desperately wanted to appear tough to the people watching us. I was still happy to be there doing what we were doing, so there is no way in which my consent was violated, but suddenly I wasn't thinking about the party or the people anymore. All I could think about was how I'd been feeling ambiguously upset in the prior months, and that pent-up sorrow came spilling out of me. Suddenly the woman's blows became particularly sharp, and clarity gripped me. In that moment I understood what was really bothering me, the true source of my sadness, and I could finally cry over it. When the scene ended, I felt lighter. That ache was no longer pressing on me, but was a known entity that I could face and work through.

It would take many more years of personal growth and understanding for me to recognize that I wanted to be able to offer to others that same moment of catharsis and revelation that helped me heal in ways I hadn't even known I'd needed. A significant piece of that discovery involved my journey through kink. I saw people find clarity in the throes of pain, and remembered my own past. Nearly a decade after my experience under the flogger, I was asked to flog others during the ritual described in the introduction, "The Scourge and the Kiss". The entire experience was incredibly powerful; I felt as though I'd discovered a piece of myself I hadn't known I'd been missing. I left that ritual with a passion for catharsis, and dedicated myself to learning as much as I could about it.

Several years more after that ritual, I was introduced to a woman who had recently broken up with her boyfriend, and was still struggling with her loss. She asked me if I would be willing to help her achieve catharsis, and I happily agreed. By this point I had trained under the guidance of others, and practiced with friends who were willing (and usually quite happy!) to be my guinea pig, but this would be my first time using those skills on a relative stranger. As I talked her through accepting herself as a being worthy of love, respect, and happiness, I felt myself come full circle, and knew I was doing exactly the work I wanted to do.

Sometimes the mechanism of catharsis is not physical sensation, but rather the emotional intensity or significance of a particular experience. For example, confronting a phobia can be seen as a cathartic ordeal if the end result is some relief from feelings of intense fear. Fear itself can be a heavy burden, especially when that fear is largely unknown. One seeker with a fear of bugs faced an ordeal in which she had to hold an earthworm in her hand. She was still afraid of bugs when the ordeal was over, but it had become a known fear, which felt easier for her to endure. The ordeal was not a cure, but releasing the intensity of that fear was still cathartic.

Punishment, physical or otherwise, can be another vehicle for catharsis. A seeker burdened by guilt can find it easier to let go of that emotion when they feel they have earned forgiveness of themselves. Punishment ordeals, however, very often wander into categories other than catharsis. In order for the experience to qualify as an ordeal, the seeker must face their feelings of guilt without any expectation of what the punishment will get them. Perhaps they will pay the price and not feel guilty anymore, achieving catharsis, or perhaps they will discover that some burdens cannot be sold away, or perhaps they will learn that there was nothing to pay for after all. These other outcomes might still be called cathartic in that the seeker will be rid of old ways of thinking about their guilt, but one could argue that the more important attribute is the discovery. Keep in mind, however, that all of these outcomes focus on the internal state of the seeker. Pursuing forgiveness from another person is an endeavor beyond the scope of this book. Shedding guilt through catharsis offers one possible avenue by which an individual might find forgiveness within themselves.

Facing past trauma and abuse can be another type of cathartic ordeal. Some seekers and facilitators use pre-negotiated and carefully planned encounters as a way to face and work through various forms of trauma. The most crucial element of these ordeals is the outcome or ending of the experience. Simply revisiting trauma exactly as it happened can do more harm than good, retraumatizing the seeker rather than helping them heal. In order for such an ordeal to be helpful or constructive, the seeker must be able to take action or find resolution in a way that they were not able to when their trauma occurred. Empowered by their ability to change their experience, what the seeker then releases in catharsis is their state of hyper- or hypoarousal.

One ordeal facilitator with whom I studied played the part of a seeker's childhood bully: he wore the same types of clothes the bully had worn, and yelled the same slurs at the seeker while assaulting him in the same way the bully had. The seeker, who had never been able to fight back as a child, finally stood up for himself and fought off his abuser. The seeker left his helplessness behind, and walked away feeling that he has the power to fight back.

We must remind ourselves, however, that even the most successful ordeals do not "fix" the seeker. Any ordeal ritual or intentional ordeal experience must be understood by both seeker and facilitator as one step along a greater journey. This is especially true of cathartic ordeals, where the entire point is to remove those things that prevent us from seeing our true selves. When catharsis is complete, we must face the self we have unveiled.

The person who fought back against their bully was able to rewrite a physical memory of helplessness, creating a new ending to their story in which they claimed their power. Nevertheless, personal growth and healing won't just end there. Without the shame of powerlessness holding them back, perhaps that seeker can now delve into deeper issues around the role of physical violence in their life. A careless or negligent approach to the mental and emotional aftercare necessary for such an ordeal experience could create an entirely new set of personal obstacles: what if the seeker begins to fear that they became the bully they hated? Contextualizing their ordeal as one piece of a complex process can allow the seeker to reframe their actions constructively; they needed to feel that they *could* fight to protect themselves, but that doesn't mean violence is their *only* power.

Sometimes the thing that needs to be released during catharsis is not what anyone expects. Seekers can have a general sense of what is bothering them, but still not really know *why* it bothers them, or what they really want to do about it. Sometimes the thing they think is the problem is just symptomatic of another issue entirely.

Once a man came to me for catharsis relating to his employment. He had planned to open his own business, but the actions of another individual left him without the financial means to do so. He felt tremendous anger and frustration, and wanted to release those negative feelings towards that other person. However, in the midst of his ordeal he discovered that he wasn't really so angry at that other person. The true source of his rage was losing his dream of starting his own business, and in order to move on to a happier and better life, he needed to let go of that dream. Only then would he be able to accept his life as it was in that moment, and plan a way forward to a new future he wanted.

When a facilitator engages in dialogue with a seeker during catharsis, they must be careful not to lead or push the seeker towards the solution they expect or believe to be correct. Instead they must let the seeker decide what their own answer is, using open-ended questions to help them see their own heart. The facilitator's job is to shed light on the seeker's path, not create it.

One woman came to me wanting to release feelings of anger, hurt, and frustration around her family. As I guided her through her ordeal, I asked her if she needed those feelings, hoping to prompt her to recognize them as something she could cast away. I expected her to find a moment of epiphany in realizing that she didn't have to carry her family's baggage if she didn't want to. Instead she clung to those feelings, and I heard in her a need for validation. I challenged that need, drawing it out for her to confront. Her true epiphany came in recognizing that she has a right to her own emotions, and does not need to be ashamed of them. What she released in catharsis was that shame.

Expectations are impossible to avoid entirely, however hard we may try to do so. Our brains are constantly creating and adapting schemas, concepts about how the world works and what creates which effect. For ordeal work we must recognize this tendency within our own minds, vigilantly watch for these moments of expectation, and firmly set them aside. Had I pushed the woman described above towards the revelation I had in mind, I would not have helped empower her. I would have forced my own paradigm on her, and that could easily have caused psychological harm. Facilitators can avoid that harm by questioning the seeker, not instructing them, and by keeping those challenges open-ended. The facilitator's job is to lift the mask and hold up the mirror, but only the seeker can see the face that was hidden beneath.

Pain-based catharsis arguably falls into the gray area in which determining whether the experience qualifies as ordeal is highly subjective. For example, some people know that being hit with a cane in a particular way will give them an emotional release that they need. Some of these individuals feel that catharsis is not an ordeal, but a well-known, intentionally sought, and desired experience. Others find that emotional release to be a terrifyingly vulnerable experience, as they never quite know what will come up when they let go of the tight lid they keep on themselves; for them catharsis is very much an ordeal.

Whether or not an individual's experience of cathartic pain constitutes ordeal work depends largely upon the mindset of the seeker, and also to some degree upon how boldly one wants to draw a line between ordeal catharsis and cathartic impact. Some might argue that there is no line at all, because the experience of cathartic impact is inarticulable in and of itself. Others might argue that the necessity of intent to explore self without expectation of result draws a fine but important line between what is and isn't ordeal. I would argue that both are true, and ultimately the only person who knows if a thing was or wasn't an ordeal is the seeker themselves.

Chapter 6: Discovery

Discovery ordeals dive head-first into the inarticulable, exploring unknown aspects of self, challenging preconceptions, and empowering through insight. Whether the result is a fundamental shift in paradigm, or a strengthened conviction in what was held true before, these ordeals leave seekers with a better understanding of who they are and how they move through the world.

Ordeals of discovery can force us to ask the question: "Who am I without this?" When one aspect of our lives—be it a job, a hobby, a relationship, or whatever else—begins to eclipse the rest of our reality, we can regain a sense of balance by intentionally removing that element and seeing what is left of us beneath it. However, we tend to be deeply attached to those facets of our identity which we cling to so fiercely, and thus even just temporarily peeling them away to see what sits beneath can be a source of suffering.

While this type of ordeal is certainly achievable through intentional ritual, often we are not even entirely aware of what elements of our lives we use to define ourselves until those elements are stripped away. This particular aspect of a discovery ordeal is more frequently stumbled upon than intentionally wrought. It is a type of ordeal often thrust upon us by life itself.

An injured athlete found themselves unable to return to their sport. They felt that a part of themselves had been lost, and fell into a dark depression. At the bottom of that pit, they had to reevaluate how they defined their self-worth, and find new sources of passion in their life. They discovered that the sport itself was not what fed them, but the desire to challenge themselves in competition. They found a new sport that their body could endure, and enjoyed competing even more than before, now that they understood their fundamental need for a pursuit of physical excellence.

This type of story is not uncommon. A successful businessperson who suddenly loses their job and struggles to find another might need to reshape their concept of self, or forge a new sense of how they fit into their family now that they are no longer a breadwinner. The death of a family member can force someone to reevaluate how they move in the world without that pivotal relationship. What brings these experiences into the realm of ordeal is not some blithe pursuit of a silver lining, but acknowledging and accepting the terrible, and letting that suffering teach us something about ourselves. (For more on ordeal as a way of moving through life, see Part V: The Ordeal Path.)

A more common use of discovery in intentional ordeal is the known attempt with unknown results. Flesh hook suspension is a fairly straightforward example of this concept. The activity is very clearly laid out beforehand with all its relative risks—large gauge needles pierce specific parts of the body, and equally large hooks are then inserted via the needles. The gauge, quantity, and positioning of hooks and needles are all known to the seeker ahead of time. In a typical flesh hook suspension, the element of uncertainty necessary to create an ordeal experience lies in what being suspended will be like. Will they fly high on endorphins? Will they find revelation in agony? Will they feel connected to the universe? Will they finally find peace in being completely isolated and alone and quiet? Each of these are real descriptions from people who have been suspended by flesh hooks; every description I've ever heard has been different. The only way to know what that experience will be like is to try it. For some, hook suspension might be a fun endorphin rush, and not quite an ordeal experience as laid out in this book. For many, it is an ordeal of discovery.

Sometimes what we discover in ordeal is as much about how we relate to other people as it is about our internal experiences of ourselves. A person came to me wanting an ordeal designed to help them face their body image issues. They disliked their appearance, and felt anxious and uncomfortable in social interactions because they were afraid of what people thought about what they looked like. This person's ordeal involved stripping down to their underwear in a room full of strangers, and then standing through two rounds of commentary from those strangers.

The first round was purely objective observation—what people saw in this person's physical body. The people were instructed ahead of time to be brutally honest, and neither understate nor exaggerate. They were to describe the physical shape they saw, no more and no less. The seeker cried through this, hearing that people did, in fact, see all the physical traits which the seeker fixated on as flaws. Even so, the seeker stood still and tall, looking each person in the eye as they spoke.

The second round was subjective commentary. This time the strangers were to describe the type of person they saw standing before them. Every single person described the seeker as courageous, strong, and capable. They were moved by the seeker's willingness to confront their self-image, and the seeker's poised endurance through the first round of comments. In the end, the seeker discovered that what people saw when they looked at them was more than just the physical body they inhabited. The strangers saw a person, and that person was communicated in bearing and action more clearly than in physical shape.

The first round of brutal commentary was a necessary piece of the seeker's revelation. Certainly they had heard before that "looks aren't everything", but in a society that so highly values appearance and attractiveness, it's difficult to feel that as a real truth. In order to believe what the strangers said about their strength of character, the seeker needed to know that the strangers would tell painful truths. After enduring dispassionate descriptions of fat rolls and acne, the seeker was confident that the strangers weren't saying things just to be nice. Thus the description of seeker as an emotionally strong and beautiful being hit home in a way it could not have before.

In a sense, all ordeals can be said to possess an element of discovery, in that all ordeals involve an element of uncertainty which much be approached or confronted in some manner. Sometimes labeling an experience as one type of an ordeal or another can be difficult because multiple attributes are in play at once. For example, an ordeal designed around facing a fear can certainly be considered cathartic when the weight of that fear is partially or entirely relieved afterward. Nevertheless, that catharsis only rarely comes without the seeker also gaining some element of revelation, whether it be about themselves, about the thing they feared, or both.

One woman who was terrified of needles faced her fear during an ordeal in which needles were pushed through the skin of her forearm. She later described a sense of stark terror right up until the moment the first needle pierced her flesh, and then a feeling of giddy euphoria when she realized the sensation was not at all what she thought it would be. Afterward, her first impression was one of cathartic relief, for needles no longer frightened her. Then she began to reflect on the emotional changes she underwent during the ordeal, and realized there was more to her experience than overcoming a fear.

The discovery element of fear-based ordeals rests in the seeker exploring why they were so afraid in the first place. Once the seeker discovers the source of their terror, that source often loses the power to frighten them, or doesn't frighten them quite as much. As the woman who faced her fear of needles processed her ordeal through conversations with the facilitator, she recounted childhood memories of painful injections, with adults often ignoring or disbelieving her accounts of the pain. Over time she began to distrust people any time they said something wouldn't hurt. During her ordeal she remembered looking at the medical needles inserted just under the skin of her arm and thinking to herself, "He said it wouldn't hurt that much—and it really didn't!" In that moment, past and present finally became separate; just because her trust had been misplaced before didn't mean it always would be, and the needles that had once been associated with inevitable terrifying pain were now nothing more than a tool that could be used in many different ways.

This woman's discovery of how her past affected her present opened her eyes to the many ways in which her childhood experiences still affected her behavior as an adult. Certainly one could say that her ordeal was cathartic, in that she released her fear, but her own perspective is that the discovery was paramount in that experience. In her own words: "It's obvious that the stuff that happens when you're a kid matters, but it *felt* real after that ordeal. I *knew* it, but I didn't really *get* it until then." In discovering this truth about the impact of her past, the woman unlocked a new way to engage with her present, and her future.

Understanding alone does not always vanquish a fear, but the insight gained in discovery can be powerfully constructive even when the fear remains. If the woman mentioned above had still been afraid of needles after her ordeal, the revelation she gained through the experience still would have helped her reshape her relationship with her past. That understanding might have helped her work through her fear over time, or it might have given her a sense of peace with herself to know that she has good reason to feel how she feels. Either way, the revelation facilitates constructive change.

Ordeals designed to focus on other attributes, especially catharsis and challenge, often become ordeals of discovery when that unknown element is finally cracked open. Sometimes the element of discovery complements whatever other attributes are in play, as seen in the cathartic examples discussed previously. Discovering what needs to be released is sometimes just as important as the releasing itself.

On other occasions, the element of discovery eclipses other attributes altogether. One woman underwent an ordeal as a commitment ritual for a deity she served. She initially understood the ritual as a challenge, a test of endurance. She grit her teeth through flogging and whipping, but found pain and exhaustion catching up with her. Finally, in a moment of frustration she asked her deity for help, and suddenly the pain was gone. The rest of the trial proceeded, but she felt no further suffering, only love and support. Later she would reflect on the experience: "The whole ritual hadn't been at all about me enduring pain. It was instead about forcing me to trust my Lady, to be honest with Her, to let Her in." This discovery of how the woman's relationship with her deity could be deeper through vulnerability and trust was far more important than enduring the physical pains of the challenge. In the end, the lesson was not about being tough, but about being able to be weak.

Chapter 7: Challenge

Challenge ordeals can be described as a subset of discovery ordeals (although, as discussed above, one could argue that all ordeals fit under the umbrella of discovery). These ordeals present the seeker with a specific task or obstacle, a test with known criteria for passing or failing. The element of uncertainty that creates the ordeal experience comes in the seeker not knowing ahead of time whether or not they will succeed, or in learning what success or failure will mean for them.

On the surface, most challenge ordeals force seekers to ask themselves seemingly simple questions: "Can I endure thirty lashes from a single-tail whip?" "Will I be able to cross this bed of coals without burning my feet?" The inarticulately profound moment or transformation comes in experiencing the answer to those questions—a seeker struggling with a horrible work environment at a job they can't afford to lose might find a wellspring of strength they didn't know they had when they endure that thirtieth lash and know that they made it through. A seeker agonizing over difficult decisions might find the inner calm they need to make the right choices for themselves as they overcome their fear of fire and force themselves to walk slowly enough to let ash protect their feet from the coals. Mindfully engaging with simple questions produces profound results that transcend a simple "yes, I can," or "no, I can't".

We must be careful not to ignore the importance of that latter possibility: sometimes ending a challenge is actually success. I once facilitated a spiritual flogging ritual in which physical endurance was offered up to Artemis, a Goddess of independence and agency (among many other things). The structure of the ritual involved each person being flogged before witnesses until they chose to stop; thus each individual was in control over what they chose to offer. We had not planned for this to be an ordeal for every participant, but we were aware that it might be for some.

I was warned ahead of time that one of the participants in this ritual was a heavy masochist, someone who would happily endure huge amounts of pain, and who would be unlikely to call for me to stop no matter how hard I flogged him. He was one of those who chose to ask for an ordeal experience.

The seeker's flogging began in silence, but as the beating got heavier, I began to ask him when he would reach his limit. At first he shrugged with a sort of pride, so I asked if he even had a limit. He shrugged again, this time more uncertain of himself. We dove into a series of complex questions and short but telling answers, revealing a crushing lack of self-worth underlying a belief that he did not deserve to limit anything. I challenged him to tell me to stop, threw it at him like a gauntlet, an invitation to duel. I dared him to acknowledge his own worth. He agonized, he cried, and finally he told me to stop, so I stopped.

As the witnesses celebrated the strength it took for him to confront his feelings about himself, the seeker began to understand his worth as intrinsic to his being, not just something relative to what he could endure. The challenge of this seeker's ordeal was not to withstand the flogging, but to end it.

Just as ending a challenge can actually be a success, sometimes pushing through to completion no matter what can actually be a failure. In such a situation, the facilitator must be ready to help the seeker process their succeeding failure or failing success in a way that helps the seeker towards their initial goal.

The very first time I participated in a group ritual as a facilitator, my job was to offer seekers a challenge in which they would receive two sterile hypodermic needles crossed shallowly through their flesh. My challenge was one among many to choose from, and with help from other facilitators, the seekers would have found a reason for choosing mine by the time they came to me. My role was to hear their choice, ensure that they had come willingly and understood the risks of what they would be doing, and administer the challenge.

One of the seekers who came to my station was convinced that she needed to see me because she was afraid of needles. She thought the only "true" ordeal for her amongst the various stations offered would be the one she was afraid of, the one she definitely did not want to do. That was, she believed, the only way to test her inner strength. She sat before me, shaking as I disinfected her skin and asked her multiple times to reaffirm her choice, and I could not shake the sense that she had missed something, that she was in the wrong place at the wrong time. I conversed with her as we waited for the disinfectants to take effect, and realized that she often did what she thought was expected of her, or what she felt was necessary, without pausing to think about what she wanted or where her limits were. I came to understand that her challenge was not to accept the needles, but to refuse them, and I tried to help her understand this, drawing out the preparatory procedures as much as I could to give us more time to talk.

In the end, however, she did not waver. She chose the needles, and I gave them to her. She did not experience any catharsis from facing her fears, nor a sense of accomplishment when it was done. There was only a grit-teeth determination as she endured, and a weary exhaustion when it was over. As soon as she left my station, I called to another facilitator and explained the situation to them. The seeker had failed her challenge, but that failure could still become a constructively transformative experience if she got the necessary support and aftercare.

The other facilitator sat with her for a long while afterward, talking about her life and her choices, and why she was so willing to push herself for others while she struggled so hard to hear her own needs. Being told that she had "failed" her ordeal was a heavy blow for someone who wanted so badly live up to expectations, but that blow fell within a context offered by the facilitator, and with their support and encouragement she was able to process that failure as the true suffering of her ordeal. For her, the fear of being pierced with a needle was nothing compared to the terror of failure, and that terror prevented her from seeing what she needed for herself. Once she confronted that fear, she was able to acknowledge her own desires, and began to embrace the necessity of personal limits and self-care.

Had I simply abandoned this seeker after she left my station, nothing good would have come of her experience. At worst, I could have merely reinforced the thought patterns she'd been plagued with when she came to me—that she could and would endure whatever she needed to in order to please other people. Alerting my co-facilitator that she needed further guidance allowed us to reframe her experience so that she began to ask herself whether or not she *should* endure even when she could. Her goal had been to test her strength, and she learned that she could define her strength on her own terms.

Challenge ordeals are not always as simple as a single activity to be undertaken or endured. A long series of elaborate tasks can present a seeker with a unique set of difficulties. Sometimes these difficulties come in the form of mental or physical fatigue, and become a part of the suffering that creates the ordeal, but sometimes they set the context for a greater revelation about the nature of a seeker's struggling.

One woman who had spent two years studying, developing, and deepening her calling as a priestess decided to perform a capstone ritual representing the culmination of her processes and the solidification of her vocation. She opted to do this at a small local spiritual event where people had gathered for a different purpose, but at which an opportunity arose for individuals to pursue independent work as needed. She planned a long series of ritual tasks to complete, and had asked a single friend to help her only with parts that were physically impossible for her to do alone.

The woman did not intend for her ritual to be an ordeal, but it swiftly veered in that direction. She had told other people at the event that they were welcome to participate if they wanted to—as witnesses or drummers if they felt so inclined—but had not actually expected people to do so. As soon as she began her first task, however, a small crowd of people gathered, and she found that their drumming and chanting brought an unexpected intensity to her work.

Throughout the ritual, the presence and participation of other people lent a dimension to the woman's journey that would not have been possible otherwise. Eventually the seeker—a fiercely independent woman who resisted any form of reliance upon others—had to confront the source of her reluctance to asking for help in the first place. Certainly she had known that participation from others would have enhanced the ritual, but she did not want to ask for it because she felt it would burden the people at the event. She wanted to provide service, not require it. As the woman saw how other people participating in her ritual were enriched by the experience, she finally struggled through her feelings of self-worth, painfully acknowledging that she too deserved to get something back from the community she served. Through that internal ordeal, brought about by acknowledging the roles of other people in her series of ritual challenges, she developed a deeper understanding of her priesthood as a reciprocal relationship between herself, the Gods, and her community.

Chapter 8: Relief

Ordeals of relief bring about a temporary alleviation from intense or burdensome thoughts and emotions. In catharsis, the point of the ordeal is to release and be free from those elements. In relief, those thoughts and feelings will still exist when the ordeal is over, but the seeker experiences a period of solace through other forms of suffering.

Sometimes an emotion is too powerful to face or work through right away, yet so compelling that a seeker is unable to turn away from it. Ordeals of relief can force them to make space for themselves, creating just enough emotional distance from the issue to constructively work through it. Some issues are so complex, so tangled with various elements of who we are and how we interact with the world, that it's extremely difficult to approach them without the perspective offered from that distance.

One seeker with deep-seated fears around her appearance endured a humiliation ordeal in which she was stripped nude and criticized before an audience. She worked in a field in which her conventional attractiveness had a considerable impact on her success, and she was afraid that if she gained too much weight, her career would end. During the ordeal, the criticisms she typically inflicted upon herself were instead hurled upon her by co-facilitators, allowing those voices to become external rather than internal.

In that space of relief, where she no longer had to be the voice of her anxiety, she could see that her true fear had to do with her spiritual calling, not public perception. She didn't actually care what others said about her, but feared that she would be unable to serve the Goddess she was devoted to if she was not attractive enough to do the mundane work she'd associated with that deity. When the ordeal ended, she still had the same anxieties to contend with, but could do so with a new understanding of why they existed, and what she really wanted in the end. With the perspective afforded to her through that period of relief, she was able to do deepen her relationship with the Goddess she served, acknowledging that there are many ways to serve divinity, and that the way she had chosen was viable to people of all shapes and sizes.

The benefit of a relief ordeal can also be much simpler, and yet no less profound. In BDSM, power exchange dynamics allow partners to consensually designate one individual as in control of another. For most, this is delightful fun for everyone involved. For many, however, it also serves a psychological purpose: it can allow the person in control to experience relief from feelings of powerlessness elsewhere in their lives, and it can allow the person being controlled to experience relief from the pressure and responsibility of decision making. Similarly when life is particularly chaotic or hectically disorganized, letting someone take control, or being controlled by someone else, can also produce feelings of relief from not knowing who is in control, or if anyone is in control at all. When the power dynamic ends, or when acting outside the bounds of a persisting dynamic, everyone has just as much personal power and agency as they started with. Nothing is cathartically lost, but relief lends insight.

This type of experience begins to cross into the realm of ordeal when the process of taking or giving up that control involves suffering, and that suffering grants otherwise unattainable insight to the seeker.

I, for example, love to be in control. Ambiguity and uncertainty make me anxious, and I manage that anxiety by making reasonable predictions about what is likely to happen, and by preparing contingency plans for unexpected developments. Life, however, is often unpredictable, and I must face its inevitable uncertainties. I keep myself together by always being ready to do something about anything that might come up. If things don't go according to plan, that's all right because I'm in control and ready to act.

However, some years ago I was struggling to access an element of my spiritual self. I felt out of touch with the primal elements of my soul, and I asked a friend and colleague to design a ritual that would provoke these parts of myself so that I could better understand them. We had a sense from the beginning that this ritual might wander into the realm of ordeal, but neither of us could have predicted how we would end up there.

Ultimately, none of the planned provocations were effective. I could feel that part of myself just below the surface, almost expressed, yet somehow still held back. When I paused to examine where that restraint was coming from, I realized that my own need for control was standing in the way. I was afraid that if I opened the door to this monstrous part of myself, it would take over entirely, and I would hurt someone in a way that I—the whole of me—would not want. My overwhelming need to maintain control was keeping me from myself. My friend could provoke me all he wanted, but my self-control would not slip.

Our response to this was to bind me, and that is how the ritual became an ordeal. Our intent was to remove my worry about the safety of people around me by simply preventing me from moving. I would be incapable of harming anyone, so that concern would no longer stop me from leaning into the beastly part of myself. I swiftly found, however, that being tied up was in itself a provocation; I quickly began to feel indignant, insulted, even angry. I resented the affront to my personal power, and immediately sought other ways to challenge the people around me. I needed to assert my power, even though my body was bound.

In this particular instance, being tied up was not fun or titillating. My resentment and indignation arose from a fear of powerlessness, and before I could begin to understand my primal self as an expression of personal power, I had to confront that fear. Eventually I reached a state of relief, where I could freely express my inner monster without fear of consequence. When the ritual was over, I resumed my usual mode of self-control, but with a better understanding of my own internal dynamics. The act of relinquishing control in order to get to that relief was a painful process, and the point of suffering that began my ordeal. I could not have reached the healthy internal balance I have today without first having faced that terrifying question: What if I lose control?

This type of relief experience is not unique to those who cling to control with a white-knuckled grip. People who strive to please and serve others by constantly deferring to their wishes can face a similar sort of terror when they must make decisions themselves: What if they pick the wrong thing? What if their choice makes the other person unhappy? What if they cause a problem, or make something worse? Facing fears around the burden and consequences of control can be just as challenging as facing fears of losing control. In the end, seekers on either end emerge with a better understanding of themselves, no matter what type of dynamic they chose to live in.

Relief ordeals can also offer an opportunity for controlled expression of suppressed impulses. A business executive under constant expectation to exude an aura of confidence and competence might desperately need relief from the pressure to be professional. A few hours of silliness can be deeply therapeutic, but moving through the shame associated with acting childish can be an ordeal. When that period of relief ends, the person must take up their professional role once again, but control becomes easier after some of that pressure has been relieved.

Another example of this type of ordeal is when the seeker vents violent impulses through consensual acts of sadism. The very fact that one craves violence can be difficult for some seekers to face, so for them simply acknowledging and acting on such an impulse is an ordeal. These types of experiences tend to be ordeals of relief rather than catharsis, as acting on those impulses will not purge them from a seeker, but make them easier to bear. Understanding the nature of violent impulses and appropriately addressing their source is an entirely different matter. That work can be made easier through ordeals of relief that ease the pressure of the seeker's impulses, but relief alone cannot offer a complete solution.

Chapter 9: Offering

Giving and receiving gifts is a well-studied aspect of every human culture. The things we give to, take from, and share with one another speak volumes about who we are both as individuals and as communities. Gifts can establish, define, and deepen relationships. They can be used to mark changes in social standing, to display status, or to make amends. None of these functions are unique to ordeal. Offering ordeals examine what happens when this process of gifting or exchange involves some form of suffering.

Sometimes suffering has nothing at all to do with the gift, but the process of offering a gift becomes an ordeal through some form of adjacent suffering. For example, friend of mine decided to handcraft a birthday present for a new partner. The project seemed at first to be a relatively easy endeavor, customized with the partner's favorite colors, but my friend swiftly found that they'd chosen a much more difficult and time consuming project than they'd anticipated. After roughly sixty hours of work, my friend stopped counting how long they were spending on the piece, haggardly determined to finish it in time for their partner's birthday. As they struggled through countless hours of meticulous work, fingers and knuckles sore from the effort, they began to wonder at themselves, at why they would continue something so difficult and tedious, for someone who was—in theory—a relatively casual romantic partner. My friend eventually realized that their effort was not just a product of stubborn determination. In a fit of frustration, when a mistake had to be undone and a chunk of the project remade despite my friend's already aching hands, they nearly quit, then said to themselves, "No, you're going to finish the damn thing because you love her." This was how that person, someone who often struggles to hear and understand their own romantic feelings, discovered they had fallen in love.

Our willingness to suffer for another can teach us many valuable lessons. Sometimes revelation will come as it did for my friend, with insight about what that relationship really means. Sometimes a seeker will discover more about their relationship with themselves than anyone else. Many of us have experienced suffering through a terrible relationship, offering affection or accommodation to someone who does not reciprocate that care. A moment of ordeal can create an opportunity to see what that suffering says about the way we value ourselves. We can choose to redefine that value by changing what we are willing to offer, or by refusing to offer anything without a fair exchange.

The suffering in an offering ordeal is not always found in the thing that is being offered. Sometimes a seeker suffers through receiving a gift, even when the giving is no struggle for the other party. Consider a pocket watch that belonged to a person recently deceased, gifted to a friend by that person's widow. The widow is relieved to give the pocket watch to someone who will cherish it. She has her own grief to struggle through, but this particular offering is not a source of suffering for her. The friend, however, finds that he can no longer suppress his own grief while the pocket watch serves as a constant physical reminder of the friendship he lost. Receiving that gift becomes a source of suffering, catalyzing an ordeal experience wherein he must confront his feelings about life, death, loss, and regret.

An offering can also become an ordeal when uncertainty arises over whether or not that gift will be accepted, and the seeker's suffering is found in wrestling with fear of rejection. One of the most powerful experiences of my spiritual life happened spontaneously in a misty soccer field where I was attending college. At the time I'd been agonizing over whether Artemis had "chosen" me to follow Her, or whether I'd simply liked Her so much that I'd decided to follow Her. Patron deity relationships—the idea that a particular deity has a personal investment in an individual and guides or watches over them—was in vogue at the time among Pagans, and I spent a great deal of energy trying to figure out whether or not Artemis was my patron.

I took this issue very seriously, and eventually had to ask myself why it mattered so much. Adopted at birth, I don't look like the family I grew up with, and have been the odd one in almost every community I've ever been a part of. Growing up I was the weird unpopular kid in a family and community where being "normal" was highly prized, and as an adult I have continued to struggle with feeling like I belong. Eventually I realized that I agonized over whether or not Artemis had chosen me because I could not imagine She would want me otherwise. Walking an Artemisian spiritual path had given me a way to understand and express myself that I'd never had before, and I was terrified of losing it. Why would She want some doe-eyed fangirl following Her around?

This is what I was thinking about as I began to cross that misty field. What if She rejected me? Even though it hurt to think about, like a blade plunged and twisted in my stomach, I leaned into that question, and considered the answer: Would I walk away? Would I just stop worshiping Her, even though doing so had such an incredibly positive and productive impact on my life? Could I just abandon this facet of divinity that I'd come to love and adore? No, I realized. I couldn't. Even if she rejected me as a devotee or priestess, I would still honor Her, would still live my life according to Artemisian principles, because it's my life, and that's what I chose to do with it. I liked who I was when I followed Her, and I agreed with Her vision for the world.

Right there, in the middle of that field, I stopped and reached for Her in my mind, and told her all of that in a silent prayer. I told Her that I didn't care if She chose me or not, that I would follow Her anyway because I wanted to. I told Her that I wanted to become Her priestess someday, but that even if She rejected me, I would still honor Her, because that was what I chose to do. I committed myself to living by Her philosophy as I understood it: to seek the true nature of yourself, to be only what you are and all that you are, to value freedom, independence, agency, and expression, not just for myself, but for everyone. I chose that path not knowing if She would accept me or not, but willing to suffer rejection, because that's how much it meant to me to walk that path anyway.

Her response, for all that it came as a tremendous relief, is largely irrelevant for our purposes here. I wanted to follow a Goddess of free will and agency, and yet was agonizing over whether or not She *chose* me to follow Her. I was not able to understand the irony of that conflict until I faced my fear of rejection, for that fear had clouded my view of my own volition.

I would not come to view this experience as an ordeal until roughly fourteen years later. It was a challenging internal process to struggle through, but in the grand scheme of my life, it wasn't *that* hard. Later, as I was pondering what makes an ordeal, I realized that experiences like this must fit; they *must* count. Even those who define ordeal by measure of physical pain eventually struggle with how *much* physical pain makes something an ordeal, a struggle which becomes infinitely more difficult when we consider how much pain tolerance can vary from person to person.

I define ordeal by function, by the way it affects the seeker, by the transformation through revelation that it offers. All four core elements were present in my experience—I was suffering through fear; my mindset was focused on seeking insight; I was uncertain about whether or not I would be accepted; my intent was to understand myself through my fear and uncertainty. The impact of professing my devotion in the middle of a soccer field seems like such a small thing when I write it here, but in that moment, in the context of everything I struggled through to get there, the revelation was profound beyond words, and it continues to affect me to this day.

We must not devalue our own ordeal experiences by creating some imaginary standard of how much suffering is enough. If it hurts, and you lean into that hurt and discover something profound that helps you reshape yourself for the better, then it doesn't really matter *how much* it hurts. What matters is that you took that hurt and turned it into power. This is the essence of ordeal.

Part III
Intentional Suffering

Chapter 10: The Anatomy of Ordeal

Now that we have explored the types of transformation possible through ordeal work, let's take a closer look at the anatomy of an ordeal ritual. By examining each stage of the overall process we'll gain a better sense of how each piece combines to create a constructive challenge. This level of understanding is an essential tool for facilitators. In order to create an ordeal ritual, facilitators must know what they should plan for, how they can plan for it, what they can't plan for, and how to be ready for whatever happens.

In fact, all parties involved in an ordeal ritual will benefit from an understanding of the considerations and mechanics that go into creating one. Supporters will be more ready to give care when they better understand why that care is needed, and Witnesses will be more able to process their own experience of what they saw when they better understand the intent and care that went into creating the ritual. This analysis, then, is for everyone, even when it appears aimed at facilitators.

While this section is written in a style that addresses potential ordeal facilitators, seekers too will benefit from an analytical perspective on ordeal ritual structure. A seeker who knows the process that goes into designing an ordeal ritual will be able to offer more relevant information to their facilitator during the initial screening and negotiation process. Having a clearer idea of how that ritual is going to take shape means they are also likely to have a clearer idea of what they will need for aftercare and post-processing. Knowing and expressing these needs dramatically decreases the amount of risk in an ordeal ritual, and increases the likelihood that the seeker will positively integrate whatever they learn at their point of crisis.

Chapter 11: Safer Seeking

All ordeal rituals contain some amount of risk. The very nature of ordeal requires uncertainty, and because of that uncertainty it is impossible to eliminate risk altogether. Physical risks are the easiest to mitigate, a subject we shall cover in greater depth below. Psychological risks, on the other hand, are much more daunting, as they are deeply personal and highly unpredictable. While establishing a seeker's intent will give the facilitator a general sense of what types of psychological risks are more or less likely, there is still no way to know with certainty exactly how ordeal will play out in the seekers mind, and thus what type of psychological danger the seeker will face.

How, then, do facilitators responsibly address those psychological risks that we cannot predict? Before even beginning the process of determining intent, a facilitator must assess the resilience factors of a potential seeker.

Resilience factors are elements of a person's environment or personality that affect how they internalize and respond to stressors and traumatic events. The more resilience factors a seeker has working in their favor, the more likely they are to constructively process their experience. For the purposes of ordeal ritual, resilience factors can be roughly divided into two categories: internal and external.

Internal resilience factors will usually be more difficult for a facilitator to assess. They concern how a seeker thinks about themselves and their life, and these attributes typically reveal themselves over time through both word and action. Internal resilience factors include:

- assertiveness
- ability to make reasonable plans and follow through to completion
- self-efficacy—belief in one's own ability to make plans and follow through
- ability to live with uncertainty
- self-awareness

- ❖ optimism
- ❖ communication skills
- ❖ empathy for others
- ❖ goals and aspirations
- ❖ self-regulation
- ❖ ability to maintain a balance between independence and dependence on others
- ❖ a sense of humor
- ❖ a sense of duty (can be either duty to others or duty to one's self)
- ❖ willingness to change

Some seekers will have a strong sense of their own internal resilience factors, and will be able to relay them to the facilitator, but many will not. As you negotiate and plan an ordeal with a seeker, listen not only to what they say but also how they say it. Try to get a sense of how they think about themselves and how they go about their life. Ask questions about challenging experiences from their past, and how they dealt with those experiences after the fact.

The very last internal factor on our list—willingness to change—is the most important element for facilitators to consider when screening potential seekers. Ordeal work uses internal conflict to let people see how they must change in order to become whoever they want to be. If a person doesn't want to change in the first place, then the conflict will be perceived as traumatic rather than constructive. A facilitator must ascertain that the seeker wants to learn from their experience; they must be willing to see what awaits them in the shadows of themselves, and be ready to transform according to their own will. A facilitator cannot create this state of being within a seeker. This willingness to change must come from the seeker's own heart and mind.

Some other internal factors can be supported by the facilitator within the ordeal ritual. During the screening process, pay attention to a seeker's assertiveness, self-efficacy, optimism, and relationship with independence and dependence. These elements in particular can be boosted through careful facilitation. A person who is weak in one or two of these areas may still be a strong seeker, but they will benefit from some extra help later on.

External resilience factors are environmental elements that impact a seeker's mental, emotional, and physical state, and affect the ease or difficulty with which a seeker will process their ordeal after the ritual is over. These are usually easier to assess than internal factors, as they are concrete items a facilitator can ask about. External resilience factors include:

- ❖ the presence of positive mentors and/or role models
- ❖ meaningful relationships with others
- ❖ social support (partners, friends, family, spiritual group)
- ❖ peer group acceptance
- ❖ physical health
- ❖ mental health
- ❖ financial stability
- ❖ stable living environment
- ❖ recreation
- ❖ positive work environment
- ❖ support from a mental health professional

Note that mental and physical health are intentionally listed as external resilience factors because, for the purpose of ordeal ritual, we are best served by focusing on how these factors impact the seeker's interactions with their environment. What matters here is not whether or not the seeker can be considered "healthy", but whether or not the seeker *struggles* with their health, and whether they feel supported in that struggle. A seeker with a chronic condition that they confidently care for and feel is well supported by their community can consider their health a source of resilience, in that it is an area of their life in which they feel secure. A seeker who is ridiculed about a chronic condition, or who feels dismissed or otherwise poorly treated by their doctors, would benefit from bolstering resilience in other areas.

Very few seekers will be able to check off every single item from the list above, and one does not need the full set in order to be able to process an ordeal constructively. The more external factors working to a seeker's benefit, the less risk the seeker and the facilitator will take when engaging in an ordeal. For example, imagine a planned catharsis that suddenly becomes a discovery of long-buried trauma, requiring months or even years of follow-up work to properly address. A seeker who has to process their ordeal while also facing constant prejudice, managing countless doctor's appointments, scrambling to earn enough money to support themselves alone, and who does not have a mental health professional to help them work through their memories, can still benefit from that ordeal, but they will face a very difficult path in processing their experience. A seeker who has a supportive community, good health, a regular therapist, and a stable job with paid time off, will much more easily craft some positive change from their revelation.

Ordeal can be a powerful tool for everyone, not just people with privilege. The purpose of assessing resilience factors is not to restrict access to ordeal ritual, but rather to inform both facilitators and seekers as to how much psychological risk they must assume in attempting ordeal work. Each individual must determine for themselves how much risk they want to take.

For seekers, that means deciding how much difficulty they are willing to face, both during and after their ritual. For facilitators, that means deciding how much of a challenge they are willing to pose to the seeker. Both parties must carefully consider the internal and external resources available to the seeker before engaging in the potentially emotionally destabilizing work of ordeal. Our aim is to establish informed consent in whatever decisions we make. There is no universal wrong or right here, so long as we keep in mind that choosing not to work with a potential seeker does not mean that person is unfit for or undeserving of ordeal. Our decision is a personal choice, not an objective judgment.

In order to assess the external resilience factors of a potential seeker, consider asking the following questions:

- ❖ Who do you know that you look up to? Who inspires you?
- ❖ Who are you closest to? Do they know that you're going to attempt an ordeal ritual? How do they feel about it?

- ❖ Do you have a circle of friends, spiritual community, or other group of people who would support your process?
- ❖ How well do your friends know you? Do you feel you can be "out" about your true self?
- ❖ How is your physical health? Are there any physical activities we need to avoid? Will you need any emergency medications (e.g. rescue inhaler, epinephrine) readily available at all times?
- ❖ How is your mental health? Are there any conditions or medications we should be aware of or careful about?
- ❖ Are you worried about money or job stability? Would your job let you take time off if you needed an extra day to recoup after your ordeal?
- ❖ Do you live alone or with others? If you live with people, would they know about your ordeal? Would they be willing and able to support you in processing your experience afterward? Is there any chance you might move soon?
- ❖ What do you do for fun? How often do you take personal time to relax?
- ❖ Do you like your job? Is your work stressful? Do you feel like you take your work home with you?
- ❖ Do you see a counselor, therapist, or other mental health professional? Do they know about your desire to attempt an ordeal? Will you feel comfortable talking to them about your ritual?

This process of declaring resilience factors before an ordeal ritual is just as useful for seekers as it is for facilitators. All of us can at times get so caught up in our lives that we forget where we can turn to for help or support. As a seeker answers the questions above, they may themselves become more aware of what resources are available to them. As you read or listen to the seeker's answers, point out the areas where they are best supported. This will bring the seeker's own support structures to the forefront of their mind, encouraging them to rely on those resources should the need arise.

Chapter 12: Determining Intent

Once you are confident that a seeker has enough external resilience factors that engaging in an ordeal ritual presents a risk that is tolerable to both of you, the next step is to determine the seeker's intent. Why does this person want to attempt an ordeal? What is their goal? What do they hope to get out of the experience? The seeker's goal can function as an internal resilience factor if you encourage them to hold it firmly in mind throughout their ordeal process, from planning all the way through post-processing. Whatever they suffer, they will know it has a purpose.

As discussed above, this intent must be held without expectation. In the most general sense, the goal of an ordeal ritual should be to challenge some aspect of one's self, but that challenge must be issued without any preconception of how the resulting conflict will be resolved. In essence, you want to have a question firmly in mind, but accept that you do not yet know the answer. An ordeal ritual asks the question, and the seeker then seeks the answer. If the seeker has a preconception of what that answer will be, then getting any other answer may cause the seeker to feel as if they've somehow done their ordeal wrong, or failed entirely. They may even be unable to consider any answer other than the one they expect, and thus entirely miss the revelation right in front of them. Facilitators too must avoid these kinds of expectations. If the facilitator has a preconception of what the answer will be, then they might push the seeker in a direction that is not at all constructive to their process.

Think of the intent of the ritual as the aspect of self the seeker wants to challenge. The purpose of the ordeal is to learn more about this element of who they are. When the goal is to gain understanding, any revelation will amount to success. This both creates an environment in which the seeker is most likely to internalize their experience in a positive way, and dramatically reduces the possibility of the seeker suffering unintentional harm through failing to meet expectations.

Some seekers will have a strong sense of their own intent. These cases will be the easiest for a facilitator to work with, as determining the crux of the issue will only be a matter of stripping away preconceptions and assumptions. For example, a seeker wanting an ordeal to face his anger over a betrayal might include in his description of his goal all the details of what happened and why that made him so angry. A facilitator must look beneath those actions and rationalizations and wonder at what might be buried in the unknown, for that unknown is where the ordeal must take the seeker. The intent of the ordeal must challenge the seeker to discover why his anger is so difficult to work through. He must confront his anger and discover its true nature. By guiding the seeker with a goal that is both focused in intent and open-ended in outcome, the facilitator presents the seeker with infinite options for responding to that anger. They might decide to let it go in catharsis, or might find empowerment in validation of their emotions, or might discover a deep fear or sorrow beneath their anger that is the true vulnerability they must confront.

Some seekers will have only a vague sense of why they want to approach ordeal. They might feel a tension within themselves, or have the sense that they are on the edge of tears and don't know why, or feel that everything is more frustrating than it should be for no reason. Determining a constructive intent for these individuals will be much more difficult. The ability to communicate about their experience can improve the seeker's resilience, so developing a foundational rapport can create a pattern of communication that will continue to help the seeker throughout their process. The facilitator should encourage the seeker to write or talk about their feelings as much as possible, patiently encouraging them through any amount of hesitancy or difficulty, and positively encouraging their attempts at articulation. If speaking face to face is extremely difficult for the seeker, consider starting out with emails, then moving to phone calls as they become more comfortable, and discussing the matter in person once the very idea of communicating is less intimidating on its own.

As the seeker speaks or writes, consider both what they say and what they don't say. What do they avoid talking about, or talk around rather than stating outright? What do they repeat over and over? Once you are able to speak face to face, which you should do at least once before the ritual itself, notice how their body language shifts as they talk. When do they relax? When do they get stiff? When do they fidget, or look away? Where do the things they say and the things they do contradict one another? As you collect your observations, be careful not to develop assumptions about their significance.

For example, consider a seeker who states over and over that her husband is the most faithful partner she's ever had, and avoids talking about how he often comes home late without explanation. As tempting as it may be to suspect infidelity and design an ordeal around facing that possibility, this approach is unnecessarily limiting, and carries with it unwarranted assumption about the husband's actions. For all you know there could be road work on his usual commute that he simply never bothered to mention before. As the facilitator you have only the seeker's perspective, so your view of the situation is colored by her perception. That *perception* is what you must untangle, not the reality beneath it; reality is for the seeker to face on their own terms.

A more constructive intent for this seeker's ordeal ritual would be to challenge the importance she places on fidelity, and find out why she does not simply ask her husband why he's always out so late. What makes the subject so stressful for her? What is holding her back from questioning him? The point of noticing all these elements of how the seeker communicates is to figure out what aspect of the seeker's sense of self, or perception of the world, you must challenge in ordeal. The root of the issue in an ordeal is almost never a matter of *what*, but rather a matter of *why*.

Even when the actions of a third party are concretely known, the intent of an ordeal must focus on the internal state of the seeker. The topic a seeker proposes for the goal of an ordeal might involve the actions of a family member, a toxic work environment, betrayal from a trusted friend, or any of the countless social tangles life presents us with. An ordeal cannot be aimed at discovering what "really" happened in any such situation, nor at controlling the actions of anyone involved. What ordeal *can* offer is a greater internal awareness for the seeker, a better sense of how they truly feel and what they really want. Through this revelation, the seeker may choose their own action, or find peace with their situation as is. The point is that the ordeal offers insight, while the seeker chooses the path.

Sometimes seekers have a clear visions of what activities they want to include in an ordeal, and will name these actions as their intent. This tends to work out well only in the instance of fear-based ordeals. The seeker may well know what they are afraid of without understanding why it terrifies them. Facing that fear becomes the intent of the ordeal, although be careful to keep the emphasis on that confrontation, not on any particular outcome. The seeker might overcome their fear by the end of the ordeal, or they might learn something important about why that thing scares them; the fear may not be something they want or need to overcome at all, so make sure to create an intent for the ordeal that will support all possible resolutions.

Seekers who are not looking to face a fear but still have a strong attachment to certain actions being part of their ordeal will usually need some extra guidance to form a constructive intent. These types of seekers are often kinksters who conflate ordeal work with other types of transformational BDSM. Ordeal is only one of many ways that engagement in BDSM can be a tool for personal insight and empowerment. Sometimes seekers aren't quite sure what type of transformational kink they are seeking, so a facilitator must help them understand the options available and the nature of that choice before they can even begin establishing an intent.

Consider as an example an individual who wanted to explore their gender in an ordeal. When I asked him to describe his intent, he laid out for me in great detail a scene that involved me humiliating him by dressing him up in women's clothing and treating him like a woman. His expectations of what we would do and how we would do it were specific, right up through the end of the ritual, at which point I would console and comfort him. This, he assured me, would help him integrate femininity into his identity. After a bit of correspondence back and forth, I politely declined to facilitate for him, as my approach to ordeal is incompatible with what he wanted. There do exist talented folk who can craft such a customized interaction to the specifications of a client, and create in that space a deeply profound or transformative experience. That is, to be sure, something I personally would call sacred, but it is not what I mean when I say "ordeal". There was no uncertainty in what he wanted, no room for the unexpected, no space for revelation. The ordeal experience I offered him was one in which we would question *why* dressing in women's clothing and being treated like a woman was so humiliating for him. We would dig for the roots of his preconceptions about gender, and be ready to learn from whatever we discovered in that space. This was not what he wanted; he insisted on keeping his script, so I referred him to someone who could create the scene he wanted, as that is a skillset I do not myself possess.

Overly specific expectations are a danger not only to seekers, but to facilitators as well. Facilitating an ordeal is an act of service, so there's a tendency to think about the intent of an ordeal ritual as delivering *what* the seeker needs. This type of thinking is problematic, however, as it can lead us to push our personal solutions rather than letting seekers find their own. It also locks us into a specific course of action: seeking that predetermined "what". Instead, think about *where* the seeker needs to go, without any attachment to what they must do when they get there. Figure out what part of themselves the seeker must confront, and how to approach that aspect of self. Then you can support the seeker as they figure out for themselves what they need out of that confrontation.

Both seeker and facilitator must agree on the course you set before an ordeal ritual begins. Had I agreed to facilitate for the client described above and simply proceeded according to my own vision of ordeal, I certainly would have violated his consent, and could have caused psychological trauma. All parties *must* agree upon the fundamental purpose of an ordeal ritual. This hearkens back to our most important resilience factor: a willingness to change.

Along the same lines, just because a seeker wants to travel in a certain direction doesn't mean you must facilitate that journey. Sometimes your approach to ordeal work will be fundamentally incompatible, as was the case with myself and the person described above. It is also possible, however, that you are simply not the right facilitator for that particular journey. Each of us have certain subjects that are difficult to approach without heavy bias. Since allowing the seeker to find their own solution is so crucial to promoting positive outcomes from ordeal work, we facilitators must be careful not to project our own values onto a seeker's process. This means understanding when and where you are most biased, and thinking carefully about whether or not you should facilitate for a seeker venturing into that territory. For example, a facilitator who struggles with ongoing conflict between themselves and their sibling might not be the best choice for helping a seeker work through their feelings about family dynamics.

On the other hand, sometimes having lived through a certain type of challenge can leave a person better prepared to help someone else face it. Experience can be a useful resource, and all of us are at least a little bit biased about everything. It is extremely difficult to know when you've worked through your own issues enough to guide another without pushing your solutions on them. Can you facilitate for this person without subconsciously attempting to validate your own choices by watching them make the same ones? This is one of many reasons why support from a mental health professional is so deeply advantageous to ordeal facilitators. My therapist will not tell me who to facilitate for or who to avoid, but they can help me see where my own biases might interfere with another person's process. They give me perspective that helps me decide whether I can acknowledge my bias enough to keep it out of the seeker's way, or whether I should refer that seeker to someone with a clearer view on the issue at hand.

> Divination is an umbrella term for any sort of psychic reading (a.k.a. "fortunetelling") which attempts to gain information about a situation. Examples might be Tarot, runes, etc. Some spiritual communities use forms of divination performed by skilled members of their community on a regular and accepted basis to make decisions.

Sometimes, especially in some deeply spiritual communities where divination is accepted, people may use divination to determine whether or not an ordeal ritual should happen, or what an ordeal should include. This practice does not need to thwart the consent or agency of anyone involved if we ensure that everyone consents to the type of divination used, to how it is performed, and to letting that divination determine the ritual. Include everyone as an engaged participant in every step of the process. Let people see what the divination shows, and why the reader, as a fallible being, is interpreting those signs in the way they are. Let everyone decide if they trust that interpretation or not. Remember that even if they do trust the outcome of the reading, they may not be ready for what the divination prescribes. When we ask the Gods what work lies ahead of us, They usually answer, but sometimes that work is for right now, and sometimes that work is for later, when we are ready.

There is no secret formula to getting the right information out of a seeker to determine the best intent for their ordeal. You must actually care about helping them, from the very first moment you begin to assess their resilience factors to the very last time you check in with their progress after the fact. There is no replacement for the authenticity required in every step of this process. For a seeker to reveal the shadows of their being, they must know that you care, that you are invested in a good outcome for them, and that you will do what you can to help them become someone they want to be. As you work with your seeker to determine an intent for their ordeal ritual, let them see that everything you ask, every suggestion you make, and everywhere you stand firm about what you will or won't offer, all come from a place of caring for their well-being.

Chapter 13: Choosing the Method

With the seeker's intent clearly set as the goal for the ordeal ritual, the facilitator must now determine the best method for engaging with that intent. Several factors will impact which activities will be most effective at bringing the seeker to a state of revelatory crisis. Seeker and facilitator should discuss these factors together. Sometimes the seeker will also participate in determining the ritual activities, but often they will know only what is possible, not what is definitely included. This uncertainty can create a sense of uneasiness, a feeling of being challenged that is just as important as the challenge itself. More importantly, however, not knowing what activities the ritual will include prevents the seeker from forming expectations about how their ritual will turn out, or what those activities will be like.

The seeker's health should be the first factor a facilitator addresses when determining the method for a seeker's ordeal. As discussed above, what is easy or comfortable for one person will be an ordeal for another, and intolerable or harmful to a third. The facilitator must choose activities that will challenge their particular seeker in the right ways.

In order to accomplish this, the facilitator must collect information about the seeker's health and ability levels, and use that information to select and adjust the ordeal ritual's component activities. The facilitator must also consider how the seeker cares for their health, and how they feel about all of these factors, as ordeal is concerned with both physical and emotional challenge. A seeker faced with a physical task that is emotionally upsetting in ways unrelated to the intent of their ordeal will have a harder time working toward their goal because a portion of their emotional capacity will be allocated to coping with a poorly designed challenge. This means their ordeal ritual will be more likely to cause harm, and less likely to elicit an empowering revelation.

For example, crossing a rocky field could be a challenging physical task for a seeker who uses a cane to help them walk. A facilitator might be tempted to restrict access to the seeker's cane as a way of adjusting the difficulty of the activity, but this must be discussed with the seeker beforehand. Assistive devices should never be taken from a seeker without their prior consent. While some few individuals might find such a challenge productively difficult, particularly if their facilitator can contextualize the experience in a way that works for that seeker and their intent, many other seekers would find the act callous and insensitive, an echo of a society that already cares too little for people with mobility challenges. If you as the facilitator think removing or limiting access to an assistive device might be an appropriate challenge in an ordeal, you must discuss that possibility with your seeker. Find out how dangerous such an act would be to their physical health, and be sure they consent to that danger. Find out also how they would *feel* about having that device taken away, if it is even possible for such a thing to be a constructive experience for them, and what sort of context would be necessary to engage with that challenge respectfully. If the seeker cannot have or simply does not want their assistive device removed or restricted, choose a different challenge.

Because of the various ways uncertainty can play out in an ordeal ritual, the seeker will not always know exactly how risky the actions they take truly are. The facilitator, on the other hand, must know exactly what risks each activity poses, and be ready to respond appropriately. In this case "appropriately" should be defined according to careful negotiation between seeker and facilitator. The facilitator must learn what risks the seeker is willing to take, and ensure that whatever activities they plan do not exceed that level of risk.

In order to gain a solid understanding of the seeker's risk profile, the facilitator should invite the seeker to share whatever information they feel comfortable revealing about their physical and mental health. Some facilitators might require fully comprehensive disclosure from the seeker in order to address their own risk profile; they will not want to unintentionally expose the seeker to an unwanted risk, and thus will insist upon knowing as much as possible about the seeker's health. Other facilitators will allow seekers to reveal only so much as they feel comfortable, and then ask specific questions related to whatever activities they are considering in order to determine which are within their respective risk profiles, and which are not. There are benefits and drawbacks to each of these approaches. A full disclosure policy will feel like an invasion of privacy to seekers who do not wish to share irrelevant health information with their facilitator. On the other hand, simply asking the seeker if they have any relevant information to share is not always successful either. Allowing the seeker alone to determine what is or is not relevant could result in the facilitator unknowingly taking more risks than the seeker would have consented to. For example, a seeker with a health condition that causes them to bruise more easily might decide not to mention it, as they consider this to be a low risk with few consequences, all of which they are personally willing to accept. The facilitator, on the other hand, may not be willing to accept those consequences. Even if the seeker considers the risks to be "low", the facilitator may not consent to pose them. Unless the seeker discloses those risks and potential consequences beforehand, the facilitator cannot give informed consent to participate in the ordeal ritual.

I have found greatest success in creating consensually challenging ordeal rituals by using a middle ground between these approaches. I explain to the seeker why health information is so important for me to know as their facilitator, and encourage them to share as much as they can. I inform the seeker that I will share this information only with other facilitators involved in that ordeal, as having the entire facilitating team aware of their needs leaves us best prepared to support them. I explain my personal risk profile to the seeker, especially as it relates to any activities we might attempt. I then ask the seeker if they have any health considerations specifically relevant to those activities, or anything that might be relevant to my personal philosophy on risk-aware consent.

While this is not a fool-proof way to avoid any unintended risk, a collaborative approach to risk mitigation helps both of us feel invested in creating a constructive experience. Explaining to the seeker why I want to know what I want to know lets them see that I care for their well-being, and that my intent is to support their health, not invade their privacy. Showing this level of care also makes them more likely to be willing to engage in whatever challenges I create for them; they will know I care enough to put safety protocols in place. From my perspective as the facilitator, seeing the seeker seriously consider the questions I ask them and give me thorough answers tells me that they value my consent enough to put effort into their part of our process. It also shows me that they are willing to work for the change they seek, which is a critically important attribute for any seeker.

While I often do not tell a seeker ahead of time which activities their ordeal ritual will include, I will have selected those activities from the options the seeker consented to in our negotiation. Safety protocols must be customized to fit the risk profiles of both seeker and facilitator for each individual activity. Thus, when a seeker doesn't know which activities I've chosen for their ordeal, they won't know which safety protocols are in place either, since the latter is determined by the former. The seeker will, however, know which protocols I plan to employ for each activity should it end up being part of their ordeal, because those protocols should always involve what the seeker themselves said they would want.

A seeker with a strong sense of their own agency will be more likely to process their ordeal in a productive way. One way to support their agency is by listening to and respecting their wishes, especially when it comes to how to respond to a situation gone awry, or how to support their physical or emotional health. As you ask your seeker about their health concerns, be sure also to ask how they would want each of those concerns to be addressed. This can include specific medications to have nearby, trauma triggers to avoid, and any other physical, mental, or emotional supports that the seeker chooses for themselves. If a seeker starts having a panic attack, and you decide to comfort them with a hug when what they need is five minutes alone, you will only do harm by forcing your solution on them. Certainly you may offer suggestions if you know of coping strategies that have been beneficial for yourself or others, but be ready to accept that the seeker might not appreciate those strategies. Respect them by respecting their choices.

Selecting a method for an ordeal ritual without telling the seeker ahead of time what that method will be requires that the facilitator have a clear understanding of the seeker's "hard limits" and "soft limits". Hard limits are activities that the seeker absolutely does not want to attempt under any circumstances. These options must be immediately discarded, because consent is key to maintaining a seeker's willingness to change. Sticking to this rule can be frustrating and even disappointing to facilitators who are genuinely good at figuring out what a seeker doesn't want to face, but needs to confront. Remember, however, that even the best facilitators are sometimes wrong, so your conviction that an item on the list of hard limits is what the seeker really "needs" could be incorrect. Furthermore, forcing a seeker into a confrontation before they are ready for it can make an issue worse rather than better, and potentially even cause psychological trauma. The facilitator must establish willing engagement from the seeker in order to pose a constructive challenge.

If you have a comfortable and healthy rapport with your seeker, then it is possible to suggest that they might benefit from facing an item on their list of hard limits. This type of negotiation must be handled with extreme care. A facilitator who conducts the conversation poorly can unintentionally pressure a seeker into attempting more than they are truly ready for. Even if the seeker consents with their words, they will still be put in harm's way if those words were elicited under duress. Managing this type of discussion without coercion requires social awareness and emotional sensitivity on behalf of the facilitator. It is extremely difficult to do well, and few facilitators will be up to the task.

Soft limits are activities the seeker feels uncertain or uncomfortable about, but might be willing to engage with under certain circumstances. These activities are often tremendously valuable to ordeal work; they exist in a realm of discomfort and uncertainty that brings a seeker closer to revelatory crisis. Even so, soft limits alone do not make an ordeal. The facilitator must learn why an activity is a soft limit, and then use it intentionally towards the seeker's goal, but only if it is appropriate for that goal.

For example, creating an ordeal for a seeker who places caning on his list of soft limits is not as simple as forcing him to endure being caned. The facilitator must learn why

> "Caning" is a common BDSM activity in which a person is struck with a rod. The type of rod, the body part being struck, and the technique used to strike are all carefully controlled to prevent doing harm.

caning is a soft limit for him. Has he never been caned before? Is he haunted by old memories of being hit with a cane? Is he afraid of canes? Once the facilitator understands the seeker's reasoning, they must then consider how or if this can relate to the seeker's intent. If the intent of the seeker's ordeal is to face his fear of the unknown, and he is uncomfortable with canes because of corporal punishment he received as a child, caning might be a poor choice for that ritual. A caning would require the seeker to devote energy and attention to confronting deeply emotional memories of his childhood, leaving him with fewer internal resources with which to face his intent for the ordeal ritual. If, on the other hand, the seeker is afraid of being caned because he won't be in control while he's the one receiving a caning, then that might be a perfect method for forcing him to engage with uncertainty.

A facilitator's goal in employing a soft limit activity is to bring the seeker to the edge of what they can handle without crossing over into something too challenging to be constructive. Transformation through ordeal requires vulnerability, so a facilitator must help the seeker move into discomfort without recoiling away from it. A challenge too severe can cause a seeker to respond defensively, raising an emotional wall to protect themselves, or shutting down entirely. The facilitator must choose a method that is difficult enough, but not too difficult. This sweet spot is hard to find, and almost impossible to predict. Consequently a facilitator must always be prepared to adjust the component activities of an ordeal ritual to make them harder or easier depending on how challenging an activity is at any given moment.

As you discuss a seeker's soft limits, find out why they feel hesitant about each activity, and what could make them feel more secure. During the ordeal ritual, present that activity to the seeker in such a way that you can add or remove supporting factors according to how much suffering the seeker faces. For example, consider again our seeker who is afraid of not being in control while he's caned. We could make the challenge easier by giving him different canes to choose from, letting him decide what part of his body we will strike, or letting him choose how many strikes he will receive. We could make the challenge harder by restraining him, blindfolding him, or giving him earplugs so he can't even hear the strikes coming. Having all of these options ready and available leaves us prepared to create just enough challenge to elicit change, but not so much as to cause harm.

As you begin to develop a list of activities that could make a constructive method for your seeker's ordeal, consider the resources available to you. Ask yourself the following questions:

- ❖ What materials do you have available?
- ❖ What skills do you possess?
- ❖ What skills will you need?
- ❖ Who could assist you, and what skills do they have?
- ❖ What locations are available for the ritual? How big are they, and what are you allowed to do in those places?
- ❖ How soon are you planning to do this ritual? Will you have time to prepare?
- ❖ How much time do you have available for the ritual itself?

When you enter the preparation phase of your ordeal ritual, you'll need to work out in greater detail all the logistics involved in what you plan to do. For now, make sure what whatever activities you choose are at least practically feasible. For example, there's no point in considering a rope suspension if no one on your facilitating team knows how to tie, or if you have an excellent rigger but your ritual must take place in a room with no hard points safe to suspend from.

Finally, consider carefully your relationship with the seeker, and how that will affect the activities you choose. Within the BDSM community in particular, romantic partners often want to facilitate ordeals for one another. While this might seem like a good idea at first—who better to help a seeker be vulnerable in their suffering than their partner?—facilitating for a loved one is fraught with danger. A good facilitator must be able to allow a seeker to pursue their power without coloring the seeker's decisions with their own bias, and no one is more biased than a loved one.

While it would be easiest and safest for me to simply suggest that people only facilitate for relative strangers, that's not practical advice. To begin with, most communities that support ordeal work are quite small, and would rely on community vetting to determine the skill level and competency of potential facilitators. Even people who are able to find an ordeal facilitator they don't know well are still likely to be working with a friend, or a friend of a friend. It might be tempting to look at those connections as unbiased, but social dynamics can be subtly impactful, especially when we're not consciously aware of them.

More to the point, however, many people simply won't want to attempt ordeal with a stranger. Ordeal is intimate work. Many folk will choose to face the added risk of having a loved one facilitate for them because they feel the comfort of working with their own partner is worth that risk.

One potential solution is to include both partners and relative strangers on a facilitating team. An unbiased third party can provide a useful balance to a facilitator who has a close relationship with the seeker. However, this measure does not address the other problem involved with facilitating for someone close to you: what if the ordeal changes your relationship? Or, even worse, what if the ordeal goes wrong, and someone gets hurt? Are you and your partner willing to accept that your relationship could be permanently damaged or even ended if the ordeal goes awry? Do you have a plan for how you could work to repair that relationship, or heal from any unintentional damage done?

There is no objectively wrong or right choice here. Each seeker and each facilitator must evaluate the risks involved according to their own standards. An ethical choice is one made with all parties aware of and informed about the risks they choose to take.

To evaluate the risks involved with facilitating for a friend or loved one, begin by asking yourself the following questions:

- ❖ Is my relationship with my partner in any way related to their intent?
- ❖ Do I understand my own bias well enough to prevent myself from forcing it on the seeker?

- Is there someone on the facilitating team who does not share my biases? Will I be able to listen to them if they tell me to back off or change my approach?
- Will I be able to watch my partner suffer as much as they need to? Will I be tempted to offer assistance too soon, or make things too easy?
- Do I have any ulterior motives in wanting to facilitate for my partner? Am I too possessive to place them under the care of another facilitator? Do I fear a sense of inadequacy if I can't provide this experience for them?
- Who will support me if my partner and I both need help processing the ordeal at the same time?
- Will I be able to support my partner at all while I'm working through my own experience of what it was like to facilitate for them?
- How could our relationship change if something goes wrong?
- If the ordeal does change our relationship, how would we handle it?
- How risky does this choice feel to me?

To evaluate the risks involved with choosing a friend or loved one as your facilitator, begin by asking yourself the following questions:

- Is my relationship with my partner in any way related to my intent?
- Would I feel comfortable working with a stranger in addition to my partner?
- Who will support me if my partner and I both need help processing the ordeal at the same time?
- Will I be able to feel comforted and supported by the same person who facilitated my suffering?
- How could our relationship change if something goes wrong?
- If the ordeal does change our relationship, how would we handle it?
- How risky does this choice feel to me?

Discuss your answers with each other. Do you both weigh the risk of working together equally, or does one of you feel that it's more or less likely to cause a problem? Do you share a plan for how to cope with unintended consequences? Take extra care in laying groundwork for constructive communication during the ordeal, and decide how you will handle conflict resolution after the ordeal should plans go awry.

Chapter 14: Foundations for Communication

While communication and conflict resolution will be particularly sensitive areas for romantic partners who choose to work together, all ordeal seekers and facilitators will need these foundations for healthy communication. Ordeal plunges us into the unknown, and no matter how well you usually communicate, articulating your experience of that process will be tremendously challenging. Facilitators must establish a plan for how they and the seeker will share information during the ordeal ritual, how they will follow up with one another afterward, and what they will do in case something goes wrong.

Willingness to change is the most important resilience factor for a seeker in an ordeal ritual, and a facilitator must carefully monitor, protect, and support this element of the seeker's mindset. In order to accomplish this task, a facilitator must find out how the seeker can communicate their state of consent while an ordeal is ongoing, even and especially when a critical piece of the ordeal involves testing their limits.

Evaluating consent for an ordeal requires recognizing that consent is not an object exchanged in a transaction between individuals, but rather a state of being. You as the facilitator must know how to evaluate the state of the seeker's consent at all times so that you can appropriately adjust the ordeal experience as it unfolds. While the seeker can and must consent to engaging with ordeal in the first place, that consent can only be informed insofar as the seeker must know that the experience of ordeal is, by definition, uncertain. It is impossible for a facilitator to disclose everything ahead of time because the facilitator simply can't know what that "everything" will include when it comes to subjective experiences. Even when the physical components of the ritual are planned out in advance, the only way for the seeker to find out what the ordeal will really be like is for them to experience it. Thus the facilitator must constantly communicate with the seeker in order to assess the seeker's experience of the ordeal, for the facilitator will use this information to make the crucial adjustments that keep the ritual in the realm of mutual consent and constructive challenge.

Communication during an ordeal ritual can consist of both verbal and nonverbal cues, and a good communication plan will include both types. This will give the seeker a wide vocabulary with which to express themselves, and will give the facilitator as many ways as possible to gauge the seeker's internal state.

Verbal communication refers to the words you use, and can include spoken language, sign language (e.g. ASL), and safewords or other coded phrases. Direct verbal communication is the easiest way for a facilitator to assess the seeker's state of consent, but it will not always be the easiest way for a seeker to communicate it. Finding the right words to articulate one's state requires a declarative awareness that will become increasingly difficult as the ordeal progresses. Sign languages such as ASL are included in verbal communication because whether you're trying to come up with the right signs to use or the right words to say, you're still engaging in the same declarative process. As the ordeal becomes more emotionally intense, the seeker may struggle to find the right words to describe what they're experiencing.

Sometimes this struggle is a necessary part of the ordeal. A seeker may need the challenge of articulating what they learn about themselves in the depths of their experience, or the ordeal itself may concern how they express themselves, or how words have impacted their identity. For others, however, the process of searching for the right words may draw them out of the headspace they need to get the most out of their ordeal experience. A facilitator should consider the seeker's intent in engaging with ordeal, as well as the method they plan to employ, and consider how much direct verbal communication they are likely to use.

When an ordeal will involve elements of roleplay, or recreate an experience from the seeker's past, designating special phrases with specific meanings can be a way to allow for verbal communication without breaking character. Facilitator and seeker should be aware, however, that the more intense the ordeal becomes, the easier it may be for the seeker to get lost in the moment of their experience and forget their special phrases. For example, if a seeker wanted to face her memories of being teased and bullied during a childhood sleepover, she and her facilitator could agree that her saying "I'm not tired yet" means everything is going well and the ordeal can continue, while "I'm getting sleepy" means the experience is becoming more challenging and the facilitator should tread carefully to avoid pushing too far. This plan will work well so long as the seeker is not so emotionally distraught that she can't remember the right phrase to use to express what she needs. Ordeal rituals are often aimed at guiding seekers to exactly that emotionally charged state, so an adequate communication plan needs to include what to do when that state is reached, and words fail.

Any ordeal that includes coded language should also use a safeword—a unique agreed-upon word indicating that the seeker wants to end the ordeal immediately. A seeker must be able to stop their ordeal if and when they choose to do so. Facilitators must remember that pushing a challenge beyond a seeker's willingness to change is extremely likely to create trauma. Furthermore, giving the seeker a way to end the experience whenever they choose supports their agency. A seeker with a strong sense of their own agency, and who is surrounded by people they trust will support their agency, will be more resilient, and thus more likely to integrate their suffering in constructive ways. If you try to pressure a seeker to let you push them as far as *you* think they need to go rather than respecting their stated limits, you not only tread dangerously close to violating their consent, but also shorten the distance you *can* push before you cause damage. If you empower the seeker to tell you when they're done being pushed, you will almost certainly be able to push them farther, and are much less likely to cause damage.

A safeword needs to be simple and easy to remember. The quintessential favorite of the BDSM community is "red", inspired by traffic lights. This format often includes "yellow" and "green" as well, where "green" means everything is good and going well, and "yellow" usually means slow down, or check in before proceeding. Not everyone uses all three colors, however, and "red" can still be an effective safeword, even when "yellow" and "green" are not part of the plan. When a seeker has a background in kink or BDSM, "red" can be a good choice of safeword because it's likely the seeker will already be familiar with its use in that context; they won't struggle to remember it when they're in the midst of an emotional crisis.

Words such as "stop" or "end" can also be good choices if you're confident that the coded language or roleplay involved in the ordeal won't obfuscate meaning. For example, if part of the ordeal must involve the seeker telling a facilitator representing their bully to stop picking on them, using "stop" as a safeword is a poor choice. "I'm done!" or "End!" would allow the seeker to go through the experience of telling their bully to stop and finding empowerment through changing the ending of a traumatic memory, while still knowing that, if they need it, they have a tool that will rescue them from reliving that moment just as it was.

In some rare cases, a seeker may want and need a facilitator to push them past their initial instinct to quit. Handling these situations with ethical care requires several precautionary steps. First and foremost, the seeker themselves must decide without influence or coercion that this is what they want, and specifically articulate this to the facilitator.

Second, even in these situations, the seeker must still have some way to end their ordeal should they need it. When seekers ask a facilitator to push their limits, at least part of what they want to confront is the root of their own reluctance. This confrontation will require that seeker be brought to the point where their first instinct is to stop, be able to express their desire to stop, and then reconcile the part of themselves that wants to stop with part of themselves that wants to continue. The agency of the seeker is just as crucial in this process as in any other ordeal—the desire they must uncover is not that of a facilitator who will continue at their own discretion, but the truth of their own desire. The revelation of ordeal is never known until the seeker themselves uncovers it, so the point of a ritual in which the seeker asks the facilitator to push them might be discovering that their limits are not so narrow as they though, but might also be that they do deserve to have and enforce limits for no other reason than that's what they want. In order to allow for a broad range of outcomes, facilitator and seeker must create a system of communication in which the seeker can express an initial desire to stop, the facilitator can challenge that desire, and the seeker must then either reassert their desire to stop, or allow the facilitator to push them further.

One way of accomplishing this is for facilitator and seeker together to determine a certain number of times a safeword must be spoken before it means the ordeal ritual is over. For example, if the safeword for an ordeal is "red", seeker and facilitator might agree that the first two times a seeker says "red", the ordeal will continue, but the third time everything will stop immediately. Each of the first two uses of "red" should be followed by the facilitator checking in with the seeker in a way that both supports their agency and challenges them to go forward. (This process will be more thoroughly examined in *Chapter 17: Approach*.) Seeker and facilitator might also consider requiring that each use of the safeword be followed by a slow, deep breath. This would ensure that the seeker does not, in a moment of terror, simply say "redredred", thereby defeating the entire purpose of using the word repeatedly, but it will still allow them to speak "red" three times relatively quickly if they simply must end the ritual right in that moment.

Another option useful for this and many other situations is to use a safeword or specific phrase to pause the ordeal and allow the seeker and facilitator to check in with each other. For example, the seeker and facilitator could agree that the facilitator should push the limits of the seeker until the seeker says, "Please help me." Once the seeker says those words, the facilitator stops what they are doing to listen to what the seeker needs, and immediately accepts everything that the seeker says after that phrase. This not only allows the facilitator to push up to the edge of the seeker's comfort while preserving their agency, but also allows facilitator and seeker a way to communicate other important pieces of information as they come up. The seeker could say, "Please help me—I need to stop," or they could say, "Please help me—sitting in this grass is making me itch so much I can't focus on what we're doing!" This type of protocol requires a facilitator and seeker who are confident in their capacity to communicate in the heat of the moment, but allows more room for adjustment for those who feel comfortable doing so.

The ultimate goal here is to create a protocol that will push the seeker's personal boundaries while simultaneously prioritizing their consent. These types of protocols, however, are best suited for ordeal rituals that take place in private locations, as public kink and BDSM spaces often have community safewords, and these rules must be observed at all times, ordeal ritual or not. (For further discussion on choosing a location for an ordeal ritual, see *Chapter 16: Ritual Preparation*.)

Finally, an ordeal ritual designed to push the seeker in this way requires that seeker and facilitator have enough trust between them that they are both willing to accept the inherent risks involved. A seeker might not be willing to attempt this work with a facilitator they've only just met, no matter how many glowing references that facilitator can provide. On the other hand, they may be entirely willing to attempt it with their closest friend, or with their spouse of 15 years. The facilitator's consent also matters; a facilitator may not be willing to risk testing the limits of someone they don't know, and such caution is wise. Sometimes this concern can be addressed by the seeker choosing a close friend to help the facilitator interpret their responses during the ordeal. However, some facilitators simply won't be comfortable with the risks involved in this type of protocol. If the seeker is adamant that this type of pushing is what they want and need despite the facilitator's discomfort, then the facilitator should hold fast their own boundaries, and instruct the seeker to work with a different facilitator.

Nonverbal communication refers to body language, simple gestures, tone of voice, and other physical cues that can convey the seeker's internal state. These indicators are not articulate, but can convey as much information as a well crafted sentence. The primary danger in relying upon nonverbal communication, however, rests in our ability to interpret it. To begin with, some folk are incredibly skilled at reading these subtle cues, while others lack the ability entirely. Further complicating the matter is the fact that nonverbal communication is not a universal language. Every element of a person's life, from cultural background to individual perspective, can influence what meanings they attach to both conscious and subconscious nonverbal cues.

Futhermore, nonverbal communication expresses the subconscious mind as well as the conscious mind. Ordeal ritual digs into the spaces where our conscious and subconscious minds are in conflict with one another. Through suffering we seek harmony between these dissonant elements of ourselves. A seeker's consent, however, must be a conscious choice. The resilience created by consent arises from a sense of agency, which the facilitator must support by carrying out the seeker's conscious choices. A facilitator relying on nonverbal cues alone, without any previous negotiation regarding use or significance, will have no idea which cues stem from the seeker's conscious versus unconscious minds. They will thus be unable to determine if the seeker's apparent consent is a conscious choice, or if their subconscious mind is leaning in a direction where their conscious mind is not yet ready to go.

All that said, nonverbal communication is still a valuable tool in ordeal ritual, and must not be discarded entirely. Before the ordeal ritual begins, seeker and facilitator must decide together which nonverbal cues should be considered conscious signals, and which are not. Subconscious cues can still give the facilitator some information about the seeker's internal state, but should not be considered indicators of consent.

The seeker must describe and communicate their own list of conscious nonverbal cues. A very observant facilitator may well have a solid sense of what a seeker physically does when they are happy or unhappy, and a facilitator with a close personal relationship with their seeker might be intimately familiar with all their little tells, but these types of facilitators still need to know which nonverbal cues the seeker is consciously aware of. Again, the point here is to evaluate conscious choice in order to establish consent, support agency, and build resilience.

The precise nature of conscious nonverbal cues can vary widely depending on both individual preference and bodily awareness. Because ordeal ritual often delivers us to a state that is profound beyond words, it is wise to prepare some sort of gesture to use as a way of checking in should the seeker have difficulty producing language. This could be as simple as a thumbs up to continue or thumbs down to stop. Using widely familiar gestures such as these is a wise choice when the seeker has no other gestures they feel personally attached to, because they will be easy for the seeker to remember in the heat of the moment. When an ordeal is likely to be extremely physically challenging, consider giving the seeker an object to hold during the ritual. Negotiate ahead of time what you should do if the seeker drops the object; should you pause and check on them, or does that mean they want to stop the ordeal entirely? An object held in the hand and dropped as a "stop" gesture is particularly useful for physically taxing ordeals, because sometimes a person's will to endure can outlast their physical capacity. Whether the issue is a shift in consent or sheer physical exhaustion, the object will alert you that some sort of change is necessary.

As you discuss what types of communication to use with your seeker, remember that evaluating the seeker's state of consent is only half the purpose of that communication, albeit the most important half. Communication will also be your tool for figuring out where the seeker is on their inner journey, and in which direction they need to travel in order to move towards their goal. Collaborate with your seeker to create a communication plan that will not only help you ensure that the seeker is constantly willing to engage with their ordeal, but that will also help you understand what they're going through. The seeker's heart is like a vast sea, and together you will sail into one of its raging storms. Without stars or landmarks to guide you, communication becomes your compass, so that you may keep the ship pointed toward the seeker's intent.

Seekers and facilitators must also decide how they will communicate with one another after the ritual is over. The process of reflecting on an experience helps a seeker integrate the profound unspeakable revelations gained through ordeal into a conscious way of understanding and moving through life. That integration does not happen immediately; rather it is the result of internal work that continues long after the ritual ends. Ordeal rituals break down barriers that prevent seekers from doing this work, but they don't *complete* the work. Seeker and facilitator both should be aware of and ready for the longer process of integration that must follow an ordeal ritual.

Hearing the post-ritual perspectives of a seeker is immeasurably valuable to a facilitator's continuing education. The immediate outcome of an ordeal is almost never the full outcome. In order to truly understand the strengths and weaknesses of our facilitating work, we must hear the seeker's perspective, learn about their experience of the ritual, and use that information to direct our personal development.

Sometimes seekers and facilitators will want to share some immediate processing as soon as the ritual is over. These first impressions can provide valuable insight, so when all parties are able, facilitating this exchange is well worth the effort. Validating the seeker's experience through listening to and accepting their retelling of what happened can also boost their resilience. It is important, however, to remember that these are just first impressions. The moments immediately following an ordeal ritual are usually not the best time for in-depth analysis. Seeker and facilitator should feel encouraged to talk about their experience, and perhaps even write about it so that they can look back on that writing later on, but both parties should take time to eat, drink, and sleep before digging into the deeper levels of post-processing.

Both facilitators and seekers will benefit from this time and space to reflect before attempting to fully articulate what happened, how it felt, or what they learned. That said, not knowing when a facilitator will reach out to check in can be anxiety producing for a seeker trying to process what was a very difficult ordeal, just as not knowing how much aid or attention a seeker will want can be quite stressful for a facilitator still recovering from the energy they put into creating the ritual. An easy solution to is to plan your post-ritual communication in advance. The following questions can guide your planning process:

- ❖ Do you want to share immediate first impressions? Would you prefer face to face conversation? Would you prefer to write down your impressions and let the other party read what you wrote?
- ❖ When would you like your first post-ritual check in to happen? The next day? A week later? A month later?
- ❖ How would you like that communication to happen? Email? Phone call? Text messages? Meeting in person?
- ❖ If you plan to communicate in real-time, how long would you like those check-ins to last? Thirty minutes? An hour? An afternoon?
- ❖ How long after the ritual would you like to continue checking in? A month? Six months? A year?

- How often would you like to check in? Daily? Weekly? Monthly? Will you want a few weeks to process alone first, and then check in weekly after that? Will you want more frequent check-ins immediately following the ritual, with updates only every other month after that?

One strong piece of advice I like to share with both facilitators and seekers alike is to wait at least a month before posting about an ordeal experience on the internet. First impressions are sometimes extremely volatile, and the internet is often not the best media through which to discuss heavily charged subjects. If you desperately feel you need to voice your experience on a blog or a website, then go ahead and write that post whenever you like, but save it rather than posting it immediately. If you need to be heard right then and there, talk to your therapist, your friends, your partners, or whoever else agreed to support your process. Just save the blog post for later. After a month has passed, read it again, and see if you still agree with your first impression. If you do, you can post it then, and you've lost nothing by waiting. If your thoughts have changed, looking back on that post might give you some valuable insight as to how your internal landscape is shifting. Either way, you win.

The point here is not to silence people who are harmed by unethical or irresponsible facilitators. To be clear, facilitators should not try to prevent seekers from posting if they choose to do so. Rather, I am encouraging both seekers and facilitators to wait of their own accord, and find out what they can learn by giving themselves some time to reflect. A hasty post can cause just as much harm to the author as to the subject, so regardless of your role in the ritual, waiting is in your best interest.

All ordeal rituals, no matter how clearly negotiated, and no matter how well planned, have a chance of going wrong. The very nature of ordeal entails that nothing is certain. We take as many measures as possible to ensure that constructive change in some direction is as likely as it can possibly be, but there is always a chance that an incorrect assumption, a poor prediction, or a simple mistake, could lead to psychological harm.

Since we cannot entirely eliminate the risk of psychological harm, we must instead create a plan for healing should harm occur. Such a healing process must provide for the wants and needs of the person harmed – for our purposes, the seeker. In an ordeal ritual those needs are almost impossible to predict ahead of time. What we can prepare ahead of time is a communication plan for how the seeker can express their wants and needs so that the facilitator can appropriately respond to them. Each individual seeker will need their own healing communication plan, influenced both by their personal communication style, as well as by their relationship with their facilitator. As you create a healing communication plan with your seeker, consider asking the following questions:

- ❖ If the ritual goes awry, are you willing to attempt communicating directly with me about what went wrong?
- ❖ Would you prefer to communicate face to face? Via text? Via email? Via phone?
- ❖ Can we use the same timeline we planned for our communication if everything went well, or would we need to adjust our pacing?
- ❖ If you are unwilling or unable to communicate directly with me about what happened, who could serve as an intermediary?
- ❖ Would you be open to letting the intermediary carry messages between us?
- ❖ If you do not wish to hear from me at all, could the intermediary still give me information about what went wrong?

Unintentionally causing harm will be emotionally distressing for an ethical facilitator. Understanding what mistake you made and how to prevent yourself from making it again will be part of your development process as a facilitator. Helping your seeker recover from harm will aid your emotional healing as a compassionate being. This might seem impossible when what the seeker wants is to be left alone, but you must remember that you will not help the seeker by forcing what you want, or what you think they need. If they wish to be left alone, then leaving them alone is how you help.

In these cases, designating a third party to convey information between you and the seeker can be an invaluable tool for both of you. That third person could give you information about what went wrong and why, so that you don't make the same mistake again, but does not need to relay anything at all from you to the seeker if the seeker does not want contact (just make sure that person consents to providing this service). Giving the seeker time and space to heal on their own terms might mean that they feel more willing to reach out directly later on, in which case the third party could indicate that they are ready to speak with you. Even if they don't, however, respecting their wish by staying away from them is the best way you can show that you do care about their well being, and that you value their consent.

Creating this healing communication plan before the ordeal ritual begins is critical to its effectiveness. Decide how you will share information, or who will carry it, when both of you feel confident that the goal is to create a constructive experience. Sow the seed of mutual respect with the way you go about negotiating this plan. Every protocol should be aimed at healing any potential wounds. I have witnessed some individuals negotiate protocols designed to "prove" that all parties consented, and therefore nothing anyone did could be wrong. This sort of thinking leads us directly into failure, as the protocols that emerge from it are not aimed at establishing and protecting consent, but at protecting reputation. Our goal as ordeal facilitators must be to elicit constructive change in the seeker, so that they may transform themselves on their own terms. If we unintentionally cause harm, the seeker's ultimate well-being must still be at the forefront of minds, and must direct how we respond.

Chapter 15: Planning Aftercare

Ordeal ritual inevitably carries both seekers and facilitators into an altered state of being. Our minds, bodies, and spirits perceive and interact with the world around us in different ways. This difference has a similar function to breaking up hard-packed dirt so that newly planted seeds can take root in that soil: it loosens us up so that solutions previously inconceivable can blossom into sources of personal power. However, this type of openness would not serve us in the mundane world. We don't want any random seed taking root in our soil any more than we want our facilitators planning out our gardens for us. (Remember, the seeker must decide what they need to grow.) Consequently, when an ordeal ritual is over, seekers and facilitators both must take steps to regain their normal state of being.

"Aftercare" is a term used in the BDSM community to describe resources and activities that help someone reclaim that normal state. Of course, everyone's "normal" is different, and the ways in which people reach their own personal normal are likewise diverse. That said, there are a few activities that tend to work well for most people.

Eating and drinking are about as close as one can get to universally good choices for aftercare. Ordeal rituals are challenging by default, and whether that challenge is physical or psychological, replenishing your body's fuel will aid recovery. What type of food you eat should be selected according to your own dietary needs and preferences. Salty foods, for example, are excellent for assisting with energetic grounding, but dill pickles or potato chips would be a poor choice for someone who needs to limit their sodium intake. A seeker who is exhausted after an especially long and physically taxing ordeal might need a snack that can quickly raise their blood sugar levels, but if they have type 2 diabetes, a spoonful of peanut butter might be a better choice than a candy bar.

Drinking water is almost always a good choice after an ordeal ritual, although other beverages such as sports drinks might be more appropriate when electrolytes are a concern. Remember that it's not just the activities of the ritual alone that will affect your body's needs. If your ritual happens outdoors in the afternoon on a hot, sunny day, everyone involved is likely to sweat enough that hydration and electrolytes will need replenishing afterward. Caffeine and alcohol are generally wise to avoid immediately after an ordeal ritual, as they affect those same bodily systems whose balance we need to restore.

Attending to physical health is only the first step in ordeal ritual aftercare. Once immediate bodily needs are addressed, seeker and facilitator should then turn their attention to psychological needs. However, we must remember not to skip that first step of attending to basic physical needs before going straight to internal processing. Physical health impacts resilience, which in turn impacts how likely we are to find constructive meaning in our experience. On some level we are all familiar with this phenomenon; from my own experience I can think of several disagreements with my partner that became full-blown arguments because one or the other of us was hungry, or of small inconveniences that felt utterly insurmountable in the face of chronic pain. Over time my partner and I learned that certain discussions should only happen after breakfast, and I know that when things that are normally easy for me suddenly feel terrible, I should take my medication. Addressing those physical needs makes interpersonal interaction and emotional resilience more reasonable demands of my holistic being.

Methods of caring for psychological needs are tremendously personal, and will vary not only from individual to individual, but also from ritual to ritual. Seekers should consider the intent of their ordeal, what types of physical and emotional challenges are likely to come up during its course, and how they might want to be comforted afterward. For example, many people find comfort in the pleasant physical sensation of cuddling with another person, but after an ordeal ritual involving intentional over-sensitization with physical stimuli, a seeker may just want time completely alone in uninterrupted peace and quiet. Encourage your seeker to think about other times that they've faced challenging situations and recall what helped them recover afterward. While there is no guarantee that what was successful once will be so again, sometimes the familiarity of something that comforted them in the past can be its own aid in the present.

Facilitators will also need psychological aftercare. Think about what you will do during the course of the ritual, both in terms of physical actions and in terms of the emotional significance of those actions, and consider that significance for yourself and for your seeker. For example, you may not have any personal feelings about blindfolds, but blindfolding a seeker who is afraid of the dark in an ordeal where they must face their fear of the unknown can be emotionally challenging for the facilitator. How will you feel about delivering that person into their fear? If you have negotiated a protocol in which they must tell you to stop three times before you end the ordeal, how hard will it be for you to continue if they say "stop" twice? What will help you regain a normal mental and emotional state after the ordeal ritual is over?

One of the more challenging factors in planning aftercare is figuring out who will provide that care for whom. The facilitator in our example above might find that the best psychological aftercare they can receive is hearing from the seeker that the experience was, in fact, constructive for them, and that following through with their plan concerning use of the word "stop" resulted in positive change. The seeker, however, is unlikely to be able to provide that type of feedback immediately after the ordeal ends. Even if the ritual was constructive and positive in exactly those ways, the seeker is likely to require both aftercare and processing time for themselves before they are able to fully understand, never mind articulate, the ultimate significance of their experience.

This type of positive feedback from a seeker is critical to the psychological aftercare of most ethical facilitators. Since seekers will typically not be able to provide it immediately after an ordeal ritual is over, facilitators should instead create a plan that will keep them at a healthily sustainable state until the seeker is able to offer the feedback that the facilitator needs. Simple check-ins usually help a great deal; knowing that the seeker is generally OK can ease anxiety around whether or not unintentional harm was done. A basic check-in can also communicate to the seeker that, no matter what happened during the course of the ordeal, the facilitator does care about them, and that feeling of being cared for can boost their resilience as they process their ordeal. Once the facilitator sees that the seeker is, at the very least, being cared for by someone, waiting for the seeker to be in a place where they can give more detailed feedback will be less emotionally stressful. If you've planned a specific day and time to check in after the ordeal, this stress will be even further reduced.

Supporters are an invaluable resource when it comes to aftercare. Seekers and facilitators are likely to have different aftercare needs, and one way to ensure that everyone's needs are fulfilled, even when those needs are contradictory, is to delegate responsibility for that fulfillment to third parties. For example, if the facilitator needs some time alone, but the seeker needs physical comforting, have a supporter ready to cuddle with the seeker when the ritual is over. Assigning one supporter to each seeker and facilitator can ensure that everyone has some way to get help when they need it.

Consider choosing supporters who already know the people they will be caring for fairly well. A close friend or partner will have an existing rapport that will help with negotiating aftercare ahead of the ritual, and will help the supporter read subtle cues to adjust how they administer care afterward. If you need to enlist the aid of relative strangers, then have each individual spend some time getting to know their supporter before the ritual begins. At a minimum, make sure the supporter knows what the person in their care is most likely to need, and have them ready to provide for those needs. Keep in mind that providing for needs will not always mean giving them something, such as a snack or hugs, but might also mean keeping something away from them. If a seeker needs time alone, their supporter's job will be to make sure they have a space to go to, and guarding that space until they're ready for human interaction.

Sometimes seekers want or even need to receive some of what they might call aftercare directly from their facilitator. This tends to arise when the resolution for an ordeal requires some amount of validation for the seeker. For example, a seeker in a cathartic ordeal ended up discovering that he craved sensual touch and emotional intimacy, but didn't feel like he deserved it. As he released his feelings of unworthiness, he unveiled a deep sadness over the fact that he was lacking the connection he wanted. In that moment, he needed his facilitator to do more than simply witness his sadness; he needed his facilitator to validate his revelation that he was worthy of compassion. As the seeker sobbed, the facilitator held him, literally giving him a shoulder to cry on. The same person who had been striking him moments before, the very source of his pain, now became the compassionate touch he craved, all in answer to his own decision that he was worthy of that touch. This immediate physical change in response to the seeker's internal change was integral to the efficacy of the seeker's ordeal. His validation came not from hearing someone say that he was worthy, but from both emotionally and physically feeling that he was worthy.

I would encourage you as a facilitator to think of this type of care as part of the ordeal itself, rather than as part of the seeker's aftercare. The seeker may regard it as aftercare, because the challenge of their ordeal is largely over, and they will be beginning their process of integration, but your job as a facilitator is not over until that seeker is ready to transition into the care of a supporter. No matter what type of ordeal you think your ritual will create, communicate with your seeker ahead of time about what you should do if they end up needing care from you as part of their process. Do not assume that physical touch, such as described in the example above, is an appropriate choice for expressing care. Ask your seeker how they feel about touch, and what it means to them. Ask them what makes them feel cared for, and then ask if you may provide that care should the ordeal require it. Even if neither of you expect that this type of care will be necessary, ordeal is uncertain by definition, so it is best to know ahead of time what care will be welcome should the need arise.

Some facilitators simply do not like to provide intimate touch or care of any sort, even if the ordeal ritual might benefit from it, and some seekers will not want that touch or care from their facilitators, regardless of the circumstances. If you are certain that you are an appropriate choice of facilitator for a seeker, and yet still find yourself in this situation, have a supporter ready to provide that care during the ordeal itself. As we shall discuss in the next chapter, creating an aftercare space that is separate from the ordeal space can help people return to their normal state of being, and having supporters wait in that separate space can ensure that they are emotionally ready to offer support, rather than themselves getting caught up in the intensity of the ordeal. However, if you know that compassionate care between seeker and facilitator is strictly off-limits, have a supporter in the ritual space, ready to provide that care if it becomes necessary.

Chapter 16: Ritual Preparation

By this point in your design process you should have a thorough understanding your seeker's intent, a solid sense of how you will approach that intent, and a comprehensive communication plan. Now you must use all of that information to prepare the ritual structure that will create the ordeal experience your seeker is seeking.

Logistical planning and preparation can feel limiting to people accustomed to intuiting their way through sacred work. If your usual mode of creating ritual is to have a general concept and "go with the flow", then a more declarative plan might initially feel like it's locking you into a course of action that may not be right when the time comes. Remember that your plan is not meant to fence you in; your plan is a tool, and ultimately you are in control over whether or not you follow it. All facilitators must be ready and willing to adjust or even abandon their plan if an ordeal takes an unexpected turn. The plan only limits you if you let it limit you.

Treat your plan like a map. The ordeal is going to send you and the seeker into uncharted territory. You can make that journey a little bit easier, and a lot less risky, by charting out as much of the nearby landscape as possible. Eventually you will have to venture into the unmapped areas, but the map still will have helped you get to that point, and it can still help you find your bearings again when you emerge from the unknown. Creating a map with as much detail as possible will help you make more informed choices when you reach those unknown spaces and must decide how to proceed.

Start your planning by writing down your procedure—a list of everything that you, the seeker, and any other facilitators, witnesses, or supporters will physically do during the ordeal ritual. Sometimes scripting certain elements of dialogue helps flesh out this procedure, but usually facilitators need to freely converse with the seeker during the ordeal. While writing down key words or phrases might help, a full script often does not. Consider making an outline that names each significant step or action, with sub-items to clarify as necessary.

Let us consider a hypothetical example and follow its design process to create a complete ritual plan. Rina, our imaginary seeker, has been offered two different new jobs, and doesn't know which one to choose. Everyone around them has some idea, advice, or opinion, and Rina has lost touch with what they want for themselves. They were miserable in their last job, and so are terrified of making the wrong choice. Their initial intent for their ordeal was to seek a decision about which job they should take, but our conversation about the nature of ordeal work helped them broaden their perspective so that they would be better able to benefit from unexpected revelations. Now their goal is to confront their disconnect with their own desires and face whatever holds them back from making a choice.

Based on the conversations we had with Rina, we believe that a combination of predicament bondage and sensory deprivation will be the best approach for their goal. These activities are well within our risk profiles, and, given our plan for direct communication during the ordeal, we feel confident that we can contextualize these experiences as relevant to their intent. We know that extreme temperatures are challenging for Rina, but they did not list that as a hard limit, so we're going to use ice water as a symbol of the suffering they fear if they choose the wrong job. Our initial procedure looks like this:

Discovery Ordeal: What Holds Rina Back?

1) Facilitator sets context: "What choice is before you?" "What are your options?"
2) Facilitator restrains seeker in predicament position as seeker describes their choices.
3) Weight is tied to seeker's hand. Place seeker's hand above shoulder height, arm roughly 120-degree angle from body.
4) Seeker's forearm tied to bucket filled with ice water hanging on a rig over their head. If seeker lowers arm, bucket tips and ice water pours on them
5) Other facilitators appear, telling the seeker to choose one option or another.
6) Repeat seeker's pros and cons for each job.
7) Facilitator #1 finishes binding seeker.

8) Facilitator #1 questions seeker: "Why can't you choose?"
9) Facilitator #1 puts earplugs and blindfold on seeker.
10) Just before earplugs go in: "With only your own voice to consider, how will you act?"
11) Facilitators wait for seeker to move.
12) Facilitators prompt seeker to explain choice, provide validation of whatever they discovered.
13) Transition to aftercare when seeker is ready.

This basic ritual outline will serve as our starting point. We're going to begin the process of fleshing out the outline by thinking about the people we'll need to carry out our plan. Start by creating a list of roles that will need to be filled:

Roles:

- ❖ Facilitator #1
- ❖ Facilitator #2
- ❖ Facilitator #3
- ❖ Seeker Supporter
- ❖ Facilitator Supporter

Let's pretend our facilitating team consists of three people: Amelia, Ken, and Leigh. These three people can fill the facilitating roles, but we still need supporters for both Rina and the facilitators. Rina's best friend, Jack, is willing to participate as Rina's supporter, and is also ready to serve as an intermediary if something goes awry. Amelia's wife, Kate, will provide aftercare for the supporters; Kate, Amelia, Ken, and Leigh have been friends for years, and have facilitated rituals together before, so Kate is confident she can help all three of the facilitators find what they need to recover. We've asked Rina if they want witnesses present during their ordeal, and they prefer a private setting, so the facilitators are ready to act as witness if necessary.

With this information in mind, let's update our list of roles:

Roles, Revisited:
- ❖ Facilitator #1: Amelia
- ❖ Facilitator #2: Ken
- ❖ Facilitator #3: Leigh
- ❖ Seeker Supporter: Jack
- ❖ Facilitator Supporter: Kate

Next we should re-read our ritual outline while making a list of the objects, tools, and other materials we'll need to carry out our plan. Careful attention to detail is particularly helpful at this stage. Imagine yourself carrying out your plan, and then write down every single object that you and the other participants interact with. As you write down your list, think critically about each item. Do you have several options for what you could use? Are certain options better than others? Is there a specific item you need that has personal significance to the seeker? Will you be able to acquire all of these items in time for your ordeal?

As we begin to compile our list of materials we realize that vet wrap will be the best way to secure our three-pound dumbbell to Rina's hand, but we want to use a sturdy nylon rope to tie their arm to the bucket. We're a little concerned about the rope sliding around their arm, and none of us are very good at non-collapsing knots, so we decide to use a bondage cuff on one of Rina's wrists, and then tie the cuff to the bucket. Ken has leather bondage cuffs, but he doesn't want to get them wet, so we decide to use one of Leigh's nylon bondage cuffs instead.

We also need to consider materials for aftercare. Ken can't eat gluten, so we decide on rice crackers and peanuts for our

> BDSM practitioners have made an art of creating safe and comfortable restraints for play. "Bondage cuffs" are restraints that attach around the wrists, usually with metal rings to attach the wrists to a rope or other fastener. Some are padded so as not to damage wrists, or specially contoured. Vet wrap is a self-adhering veterinary-care bandage used on horses and dogs to wrap and support weak limbs. It is sometimes used for BDSM restraint.

snack food. Rina has a blanket they want to curl up in after everything is over, and we've told them to make sure they bring it with them on the day of the ritual. Ken and Leigh don't anticipate needing much aftercare, but they plan to have a snack and check in with Kate just in case. Amelia wants some quiet time alone with Kate and is content to wait until everyone else is taken care of. If things get tense, she can write in her journal while she waits, since that tends to help her settle her mind.

As we list each object we'll need for the ritual, we should also write down who is responsible for bringing that item to the ritual space. At this point, our materials list should look like this:

Materials

- Vet wrap *(Amelia)*
- Nylon rope *(Leigh)*
- Nylon cuff *(Leigh)*
- Bucket *(Amelia)*
- Suspension Rig *(Ken)*
- Ice *(Ken)*
- Water for the bucket *(Ken)*
- Blindfold *(Amelia)*
- Ear plugs *(Amelia)*
- Peanuts *(Kate)*
- Rice crackers *(Kate)*
- Cooler full of water *(Kate)*
- Cups (Kate)
- Napkins *(Kate)*
- Blanket *(Rina)*
- Journal *(Amelia)*
- Pen *(Amelia)*

Now we must consider where we will hold our ordeal ritual. Sometimes the location for a ritual will be determined early in the design process. This typically happens either when the method of the ordeal requires a specific type of environment, or when your choice of venue is limited by other factors. A common example of this from the BDSM world is the case of BDSM conventions and camping events. Many kinksters develop connections with people they only get to see on a yearly basis at these types of gatherings. If a seeker from Minnesota and a facilitator from Georgia are planning to attend the same kink event, it might make more sense for them to use that time and space for their ordeal ritual, rather than attempting to travel to one another at some other time.

> While not all BDSM practitioners want to get together in community, many enjoy going to conferences or large camping gatherings where they can learn new techniques, get support, find new friends and partners, and watch practitioners who are comfortable playing in public. At these gatherings, consent is strongly enforced and public play is never required or pressured. Ground rules are clearly stated.

Holding your ordeal ritual at a kink event will have some advantages, but also several drawbacks. The major advantage is community; kink events are populated by people who are not likely to look unfavorably upon the ritual solely because of the activities it includes. Safety from this type of judgment will create a higher capacity for emotional vulnerability in the seeker, which will help them get more out of their ordeal experience. Furthermore, if the event in question is one that the seeker attends along with many of their friends and loved ones, the presence of that community will boost their resilience, thus lowering the psychological risk of their ritual.

On the other hand, kink events are spaces meant for all attendees, not just you and your seeker. As you plan a ritual at a kink event, you will need to be mindful not only of your seeker's needs, but also of the impact your ritual will have on others. Finding a secluded corner of a campground to have your private ritual is sometimes fine, but completely taking over one of the event's public spaces is both rude and disruptive. Hotel conventions are particularly challenging in this regard, as space is typically limited to begin with. Sometimes events might be willing to add your ritual to their schedule and give you an assigned space, so it's always worth asking if that's an option. Many factors will affect the event's decision-making process, including the size of the venue, the total number of attendees, and whether or not you're willing to open the ritual for attendees to witness if they choose. If the event declines to give you a designated space, it may have nothing to do with you or your ritual, so accept their decision gracefully and seek other options.

Some people might want to hold their ritual in a public BDSM playspace. They might feel that having the ordeal in public is part of the point, or that whoever wants to watch is welcome. Please remember, however, that everyone participating in an ordeal must consent to do so, and that includes witnesses. Yes, sometimes kink scenes stumble into ordeal, but that is an entirely different matter from intentionally bringing ordeal into a public space. What is completely unremarkable for one person can be traumatically triggering for another, and in an ordeal ritual the emotional intensity alone can be challenging or even triggering for people watching. This type of risk is present in BDSM play as well, and each community has its own ways of assessing and handling that risk. Before you decide to attempt ordeal work at a kink event, think about the values of the community. An ordeal ritual in a public playspace would be a terrible choice for an event which is aimed at introductory experiences for people who are new to BDSM. If the event is aimed at kink veterans, and openly embraces more

> BDSM practitioners who enjoy playing for an audience, or who like to watch other players, or who want to use equipment they may not have at home, might attend "play parties", private events held in homes or at clubs. Again, each venue has public rules of behavior and full consent is underscored. "Dungeon monitors", people who enforce safe behavior, are common. Some parties have a "house safeword" which all are expected to use.

challenging subjects, then there might be a way for you to hold your ritual there without disrupting the event.

Whether you're at a kink event, a public venue, a person's home, or anywhere else, make sure your ritual follows the rules of wherever you are. If you're not sure whether or not the ritual you have in mind would be allowed in that space, ask the venue owners or event organizers, and get permission beforehand. Breaking the rules can endanger not only you and the people around you, but also the venue itself. Many spaces are available only so long as the people in them conform to pre-negotiated rules. If you break those rules, you risk the space for everyone.

In our hypothetical ritual example, Rina wanted a private setting. All of the people involved attend a kinky camping event, and we could, in fact, secure a private space at that event in which to hold our ritual. However, after discussing the issue as a whole group, we've decided not to use this option. Kink events tend to be very busy, with lots of classes to attend, and exciting experiences to share. The hustle and bustle of a convention are not a good fit for the goal of Rina's ordeal, and none of us on the facilitating team feel up to cramming our ritual into a busy event schedule.

Instead, Leigh has offered to let us use their back yard. They have a nice open space surrounded by a privacy fence, and they are not concerned about what their neighbors might overhear. The weather looks good for the day and time we've chosen, but we've selected a rain date just in case. Leigh has a sturdy tree growing in their back yard with a limb that would work perfectly for holding up our bucket, so Ken no longer needs to borrow a suspension rig from his friend. Instead we're going to use some nylon straps and a carabiner to hold up the bucket. We tested our setup using Amelia as a stand-in for Rina, and, with a slight adjustment to how the rope attaches to the bucket, everything works as planned.

Holding our ritual at Leigh's home also affords us several other convenient solutions. Rina wants to stay outside for their aftercare. Even though it usually helps to transition to a different space, Rina deeply enjoys open air and a view of the sky, and feels that these will help them more than changing locations. Ken and Leigh can check in with Kate in Leigh's living room, so that Rina and Jack can have the back yard to themselves once the ritual is over. Leigh has offered their bedroom as a quiet private space for Amelia to write in her journal while she waits for Kate to be available, and then she and Kate can stay there to have their time alone.

Now we can go back to our outline and materials list, and update both with this new information:

Discovery Ordeal: What Holds Rina Back?
- I. Set up.
  - A) Strap with carabiner on tree limb.
  - B) Other materials nearby.
  - C) Ropes.
    - 1) One for hoisting bucket up.
    - 2) One for predicament.
  - D) Vet wrap.
  - E) Dumbbell.
- II. Prep for aftercare.
  - A) Snacks and drinks in backyard for Rina and Jack.
  - B) Snacks and drinks in living room for Ken and Leigh.
  - C) Snack, drink, journal, and pen in bedroom for Amelia.
  - D) Jack waits in living room with Rina's blanket.
  - E) Bucket prep.
    - 1) Bucket in kitchen.
    - 2) Ice cubes in freezer.
    - 3) Water chilled in refrigerator.
- III. Ordeal begins.
  - A) Amelia sets context.
    - 1) "What choice is before you?"
    - 2) "What are your options?"
  - B) Amelia begins to restrain Rina as they describe their choices.
    - 1) Weight tied to Rina's hand.
    - 2) Cuff attached to Rina's wrist.
    - 3) Rope tied to cuff.
  - C) Ken and Leigh enter back yard carrying bucket full of ice and water.

1) Ken and Leigh place bucket between Amelia and Rina so that Rina can see its contents.
2) Amelia continues restraining Rina with help from Ken and Leigh.
3) Amelia ties ropes to bucket handle—one at center, one at edge.

D) Amelia places Rina's hand above shoulder height, arm roughly 120-degree angle from body.
1) Ken hoists bucket in place, holds it up while Leigh attaches bucket handle to carabiner that will hold it in place over Rina's head.
2) Amelia ties predicament rope to cuff on Rina's wrist.
3) If Rina lowers arm, bucket tips and ice water pours on them.

E) Amelia echoes Rina's choices.
1) "So your choices are to take the job at X, or take the job at Y." Just name them, but name them however Rina named them.
2) Ken and Leigh start telling Rina to choose one option or another.
3) Each repeat Rina's pros and cons for one of the jobs
4) Amelia questions Rina: "Why can't you choose?" Give as much time to struggle with this as Rina needs.

F) Amelia puts earplugs and blindfold on Rina.
1) Just before earplugs go in: "With only your own voice to consider, how will you act?"
2) Facilitators wait for Rina to move.
3) Rina makes their choice.
4) Facilitators prompt Rina to explain their choice, provide validation of whatever Rina discovered.

G) Transition to aftercare when Rina is ready.
1) Jack comes out to back yard, brings blanket.
2) Ken and Leigh go to living room.
3) Amelia goes to bedroom.
4) Kate checks in with Ken and Leigh.

H) Before Rina leaves Leigh's house, they or Jack will check in with Kate. Possibly also with Amelia if both feel up to it.

I) Once Rina has gone, Amelia gets time alone with Kate.

Materials

- Vet wrap *(Amelia)*
- Nylon rope *(Leigh)*
- Nylon cuff *(Leigh)*
- Bucket *(Amelia)*
- Ice *(Leigh's freezer)*
- Water for the bucket *(Leigh's kitchen)*
- Blindfold *(Amelia)*
- Ear plugs *(Amelia)*
- Peanuts *(Kate)*
- Rice crackers *(Kate)*
- Cooler full of water in the back yard *(Kate)*
- Cups (Kate)
- Napkins *(Kate)*
- Blanket *(Rina)*
- Journal *(Amelia)*
- Pen *(Amelia)*

Once you have your ritual plan pretty well laid out, take another look at it solely from the perspective of risk mitigation. Consider any new safety risks that have come up as you developed your plan, as well as everyday hazards that are easy to overlook if you focus too closely on the ritual method alone. Some of the risks you will need to address may be a result of activities intentionally chosen as part of the ordeal ritual, but even a ritual that is primarily psychological in nature, with no planned physical activities, is still vulnerable to simple accidents. Preparing for these possibilities is not just good practice; it's also another way to show the seeker that you care for their well-being, and, in doing so, build trust between you.

Discuss this updated information with your seeker, and make a plan for how to address any potential injuries. Note that what is required is a plan for care; treatment does not necessarily need to be provided by a facilitator. For example, a seeker may agree to letting their facilitator administer basic first aid, but if the seeker were instead to trip and break their leg, an appropriate response would involve getting the seeker to a qualified medical professional. Seeker and facilitator should discuss in advance what physical risks their ritual will pose, what accidents they feel they need to be ready for, and what action plan to use should any of those injuries occur.

In our hypothetical example, we've decided not to tell Rina about our ritual plan so that they won't develop too many expectations about the experience. We still need to discuss risks, though, and find out how Rina would want us to address them. We've tested our bucket system pretty well, and we're using a plastic bucket to avoid serious injury just in case it fails, but we've still got something suspended over Rina's head, so we want to make sure we find out how they would want us to respond to a possible concussion. Based on the preparatory work we've done, we think it's extremely unlikely to occur, but we still want to communicate that possibility, and make a plan to address it.

In order to communicate this possibility and gather necessary information without giving away our ritual plan, we ask Rina to consider several potential risks, many of which have nothing to do with our plan. We ask Rina how long they can run at full speed, how long they can stand in place, if they've ever passed out from holding a single position for too long, if they can do a pull up, if they can do a push up, what their favorite color is, if they've ever been stung by a bee, it they sunburn easily, and how they feel about public nudity. We intentionally throw in a silly or inconsequential question—in this case, their favorite color—as a clue that not *all* of these questions are relevant to our plan. We don't want to overwhelm Rina with too much dread; we just want them to know that we care enough about their safety to ask about their health.

As we ask Rina each of these questions, we respond to their answer with another question about how they would want to handle that particular situation if it goes sideways. For example:

Amelia: "Can you do a pull-up?"

Rina: "I don't think so. I've never tried."

Amelia: "If you slipped off the pull-up bar and fell to the ground, how would you want us to respond? Could one of us administer first aid?"

Rina: "If I just got a few scratches, sure, but if it were more serious, I think I'd want to see a professional."

Amelia: "What would be serious to you?"

Rina: "Like if I thought I broke something, or if I was bleeding a lot."

Amelia: "Ken is first-aid certified. Would you be all right with him giving you first aid?"

Rina: "Sure, but, again, only if it's not serious."

Amelia: "OK. If you're really emotionally distraught, or stressed out, or otherwise distracted, do you still want to have the final call on what's serious enough to warrant a trip to a doctor? Or would you be willing to let Jack or someone else make that call?"

Rina: "Well, if I'm unconscious, then that's serious enough! But if I'm just in a weird headspace or something, then, yeah, Jack can decide at least until I get back to a good headspace."

One thing in particular for us to pay attention to here is Rina's struggle to define what type of injury is serious enough to warrant attention from a medical professional. It is often hard enough to figure out when we need to see a doctor about our health issues even outside of an ordeal. Trying to guess what might be serious enough to require medical attention in a ritual we know very little about will inevitably be much harder. Make sure you know not only what your seeker wants so far as they can predict what might happen, but also how they would want decisions to be made if what happens falls outside of what you predicted.

During our full conversation we find two more interesting pieces of information that we'll want to take note of as we continue our ritual preparation. First, we learn that Rina gets sore knees if they stand in one place for more than about 45 minutes. We asked if this is a pain they want to avoid, or if it's something they are willing to push through if it adds to their ordeal experience. They said they could push through it up to a point, but eventually they would need to sit. We don't think this ritual is likely to run long enough for that to be a problem, and if Rina's knees motivate them to move, that could actually help our ordeal. That said, we also know that knee pain might just distract Rina, so we're going to have a chair ready just in case they need to sit before the ritual is over. Amelia is also going to practice adjusting the length of the rope attached to the cuff without spilling the bucket prematurely, so we'll be ready to make that change if it becomes necessary.

Finally, Rina reveals that they have never before been stung by a bee. We asked this question because we are holding our ritual outdoors, and even though Leigh generally doesn't get a ton of bees in the back yard, it's still something that could potentially happen. Because Rina has never been stung before, we have no idea if they are allergic to bee stings or not. We asked Rina what they would want us to do if they started to have an allergic reaction to a bee sting. The nearest emergency room is only a few minutes from Leigh's house, and Rina's health insurance is such that they are concerned about the cost of an ambulance ride, so unless a medic is absolutely required immediately on site, Rina would prefer that Jack drive them to the ER.

At this point, we have a solid ritual plan, we know what safety measures we will have in place, and we know how to figure out what to do if something unexpected happens. Now, if you're anything like me, you'll also want to have a plan B, plan C, and plan D, just in case you get to your ritual and find out that what worked well in theory falls flat in practice, or in case the suffering you thought would be just challenging enough ends up much too easy, or much too hard. You don't necessarily need to have these backup plans thoroughly fleshed out, but it does help to have an idea of what else you can do just in case you need to change course.

In our example, we want to have a backup plan just in case Rina doesn't reach an ordeal state from the predicament alone. Amelia, Ken, and Leigh have a long conversation about what they can say to Rina before the earplugs go in that might help Rina contextualize the predicament, but we are also ready to emotionally challenge Rina after the bucket spills. If Rina doesn't find a moment of clarity before pulling on the rope, we're ready to hold up their self-doubt afterward, and make them face the consequences of making a choice, no matter what choice it is.

Finally, as the day and time of your ordeal ritual approaches, all participants should engage in some type of personal psychological and spiritual preparation. This will be as individually variable as aftercare. As a facilitator I typically want to review my notes, lists, and outlines several times leading up to a ritual. This commitment to quality in my work is a spiritual act, an expression of value, and respect for the sacredness of ordeal. I also generally feel less anxious when I have more information, so the best way for me to ease pre-ritual jitters is to review the information I have. One of my colleagues is nearly the opposite—they need to have time completely off from anything related to ordeal or ritual in order for them to work effectively. As much as they enjoy facilitating ordeal rituals, they also find them extremely tiring. They do their best work when they arrive physically and mentally "fresh". Lots of review ahead of time just makes them tire out faster. As you prepare for an ordeal ritual, think about what helps you stay focused and engaged in what you're doing. You will need to give the ritual your full attention from start to finish, so prepare in whatever way will best help you accomplish that.

Seekers generally benefit from some amount of reflection leading up to their ordeal. Journaling, talking with friends, meditating, and simply spending time alone to think are all good ways to go about this reflection. Instruct your seeker to focus on whatever inner conflict they want to face in their ordeal, and do whatever they need to do to have that conflict near the front of their minds when they arrive for their ritual.

As Rina prepares for their ordeal ritual, they have one more conversation with Jack about the two jobs they must choose between. In the car on the way to Leigh's house, Rina tells Jack all about the pros and cons of each job, and recounts their miserable experiences in their last job, which seemed like it would be a great one when they took it. Rina tries to guess which of their potential new jobs is more or less likely to have the same problems, or entirely different problems, and arrives at Leigh's house for their ritual with these thoughts still circling in their mind.

Chapter 17: Approach

With a plan in hand, a space set up, and people ready to participate, it's time for the ritual itself to begin. Whether you're using high ceremony in a formal and complex plan, or setting intent behind a single simple action, facilitators must create context for the seeker's experience, and help the seeker reach a mindset that will lead to ordeal. This is your approach, the stage of the ritual in which you guide the seeker toward their intent.

The approach stage of an ordeal ritual serves as a warm-up period for the seeker. Too much suffering too quickly causes a person to shut down rather than opening up. This emotional shut-down can take the form of physically or verbally freezing, attempting to fight off the facilitators, attempting to escape the ordeal, or excessive acquiescence in an attempt to avoid conflict. All of these responses are different types of defense mechanisms automatically engaged when the intensity of an experience becomes more than a person can normally cope with.

Facilitators must help seekers maintain engagement with their ordeal by keeping pace with the seeker's capacity to suffer. Without this careful pacing, a seeker may react reflexively, trying to shut away an experience that is intolerably challenging. When an ordeal gradually increases in intensity over time, the seeker will be better able to remain constantly aware of the present moment, intentionally seeking their own strength through their suffering.

Where physical pain is involved, pacing the experience is relatively straightforward. Begin with gentler sensations, and gradually increase intensity at a rate that demands the seeker's attention, but allows that attention to be shared with the intent of their ordeal. Of course, what is appropriately "gradual" for one person will be achingly slow for another, and impossibly fast for a third. Facilitators must use the communication plan they developed with their seeker to assess the intensity of the seeker's experience and adjust their approach accordingly.

Mental, emotional, and spiritual suffering require a warm-up for similar reasons. When an experience is too intense or stressful to immediately cope with, our minds come up with many creative ways to avoid confronting the root of the issue, and yet that confrontation is exactly what we want in an ordeal experience. An ordeal ritual approach must offer the seeker just enough familiarity and comfort with the issue to allow the seeker to face it, but not so much comfort that they can avoid it. In our hypothetical example from the last chapter, Rina telling Amelia about their job choices serves as a mental warm-up. Rina revisits familiar cycles of distress as they recount the situation yet again, and that familiarity creates enough comfort to push their distress towards ordeal.

As your approach continues towards the state of crisis that will elicit transformation, everything the facilitator does must have a meaning relevant to the seeker's goal. This meaning creates context for the seeker's experience, and that context will help shape the mindset that turns the seeker's suffering into an ordeal. If necessary, meaning can be explicitly laid out by the facilitator. For example, in an ordeal using physical pain to help a seeker find his true feelings about a challenging relationship, a facilitator could question the seeker as they deal out that pain, asking things like, "How much are you willing to hurt for him?" This type of dialogue directly links physical sensation to the emotional meaning that is critical for internal transformation.

However, in many situations it is more useful to present the seeker with many possible ways to interpret their suffering rather than pushing a specific symbolism. When seekers are able to interpret their experience on their own terms, they can find revelations that might have been excluded by a more facilitator-directed approach. Also, facilitators are also less likely to project their own biases on the seeker if they let the seeker interpret their experience on their own terms. In these situations, however, the facilitator must still ensure that there is *some* context for the actions of the ritual. You can accomplish this by asking the seeker what something means to them, or by challenging them to find meaning in what they do or feel.

In our example from last chapter, we're going to use a combination of meaning explicitly laid out, and meaning to be determined by the seeker. As Rina is bound into their predicament, Amelia, Ken, and Leigh very directly call to mind Rina's job choices. The questions Amelia asks paired with the pros and cons Ken and Leigh speak for each job make the predicament a clear symbol of Rina's internal conflict over which job to take. However, when Rina is finally blindfolded and left to struggle with making a decision, the question Amelia asks before putting in earplugs is intentionally vague: "With only your own voice to consider, how will you act?" The question is not "Which will you choose?" or "How will you decide?" but "How will you act?" Amelia, Ken, and Leigh want to leave room for the possibility that the true conflict Rina must face has nothing at all to do with the job choice, but is instead a fear of unknown consequences in any choice. If there truly is one job that shines over another in the midst of Rina's ordeal, then their action can be choosing that job, and facing the bucket of ice water will be worth that choice. If the real issue is not which choice to make, but making any choice at all, then being forced to face a bucket of ice water will represent facing the unknowable future. At that point, *what* Rina chooses doesn't matter nearly as much as the fact that they choose at all. It's also possible that Rina doesn't want either of these jobs. If they discover that neither one is worth facing the ice water, their solution might be to call for Amelia to release them from the predicament; that too is an available choice. This combination of explicitly crafted symbolism with multiple possibilities for interpretation and resolution helps the Rina find their own answers, and prevents Amelia, Ken, and Leigh from pressuring Rina in any particular direction other than the one Rina chose for their intent.

Sometimes it's hard to find the issue at the root of an ordeal. Rina's example is a relatively simple one; reality won't always be that straightforward. Often a facilitator must use the approach stage of an ordeal ritual to help the seeker figure out what they must confront in the crisis stage. Plain speech is a powerful tool for this process. A facilitator can reap a wealth of information just by listening to *how* a seeker discuses a topic or answers a question. Pay attention to what the seeker avoids talking about, or what they repeat over and over. Point out those aversions and repetitions to the seeker, and ask them why they're avoiding or repeating those particular statements.

The dialogue between facilitator and seeker during the approach stage of an ordeal should function like a mirror. The facilitator reflects the seeker's own statements and assumptions back at them, being as careful as possible to avoid projecting their own biases in the process. The safest way to accomplish this is to simply repeat what the seeker says, adding questions that either challenge the seeker to confirm or deny their own statements, or that offer open-ended opportunities to elaborate on a statement.

When you challenge a seeker's statements, be careful not to imply a wrong or right answer in how you deliver the challenge. Practice challenging yourself, and listen to how the tone of your voice changes the implication of a simple question: "Is that how you really feel?" Those same words sound quite different when you raise inflection at the end of the question versus when you lower it; the former conveys interest, whereas the latter conveys skepticism. No matter how aggressively you pose your question to the seeker, make sure that your intonation conveys interest in whatever their answer truly is, so that whether they need to reaffirm their statement or modify it, they are not artificially pushed in either direction.

Open-ended questions will prompt the seeker to share more information without hinting at what that information should be. For example, if a seeker confronting their feelings about a breakup states, "I feel hurt," a facilitator might be tempted to ask "Why did the breakup hurt you?" This approach is unwise, however, because it assumes an origin for those feelings that may not be accurate. A better question would be "Why do you feel hurt?" If the source of the seeker's hurt is the breakup, they'll still be able to state that, but they'll also have the opportunity to offer much more information. Perhaps the response will be "Because I had no idea it had gotten so bad for him," or "Because I'm afraid of being alone." Each of those statements offer invaluable clues to both facilitator and seeker that might be missed if the question limited attention to only the breakup itself.

Another important function of the approach phase of an ordeal ritual is creating resilience through interaction between facilitator and seeker. As a companion on the seeker's journey, the facilitator can represent internal resilience factors that the seeker otherwise struggles with. Consider your seeker's individual resilience factors, and give them an extra boost where needed:

❖ Encouraging the seeker can provide optimism and elicit assertiveness.

- ❖ Validate the seeker's experience to help increase their self-awareness.
- ❖ Expressing faith in the seeker's capacity to complete an ordeal can counterbalance a lack of self-efficacy
- ❖ Use the established communication plan to bolster communication skills.
- ❖ Remind the seeker of their intent so that they can be motivated by their goal.
- ❖ Frequently and explicitly reestablish consent to affirm and support the seeker's agency.

There is no way to predict how long your approach will take, or what will finally catalyze the seeker's revelation. A facilitator must be ready to give the seeker as much time as they will need. Sometimes that means continuing dialogue and maintaining support through hours of discussion. At other times, as in our example of Rina's ordeal, it means leaving the seeker alone to find their own answers. Sometimes a seeker who seemed like they would require lots of interaction with the facilitator suddenly stumbles upon transformation in an entirely internal process; sometimes the internal process is not as effective as you hoped it would be, and the facilitator must offer additional guidance.

If Rina can't make a decision on their own, Amelia is ready to take out the earplugs and talk Rina through the predicament. Rina's facilitators hope that Rina will be able to find some clarity after external pressures are emphasized, and then suddenly removed. However, if Rina still struggles to decide, Amelia is ready to be the mirror, and help Rina confront their indecision.

The closer you get to the revelation at the center of an ordeal, the less predictable the experience will become. Keep your map handy so that you can always find your bearings, but be ready to cross into uncharted territory, for it is in those unknown spaces that transformation happens.

Chapter 18: Crisis

The climax of an ordeal ritual happens when the seeker recognizes what stands between them and their goal, and acknowledges the necessity of change. The seeker experiences an internal crisis, in which they must decide what to do about whatever blocks their path. Recognition of the obstacle requires radical change, whether they decide to remove the obstacle and continue forward, or decide the obstacle is a necessary feature of their inner landscape, and instead travel in a new direction. This is the point within an ordeal ritual that is most difficult to articulate, and impossible to anticipate. During the approach phase, the facilitator attempts to get the seeker as close to crisis as possible, but ultimately the seeker must recognize the obstacle, and choose their path.

As a seeker draws closer to crisis, a facilitator's job becomes more and more delicate. Sometimes the extra push a seeker needs to acknowledge the root of their struggle sits at the very edge of consent, and for all that facilitators may need to walk right up to that line, they must take care never to cross it. Once a seeker reaches their state of crisis, the facilitator must stop pushing and challenging altogether, instead holding space for the seeker to decide on their own terms how they want to resolve their crisis. It is therefore essential that a facilitator watch carefully for that point at which they must shift their interaction from a combination of pushing and supporting to one that is exclusively validating.

Every seeker will experience the crisis phase differently, so recognizing that state will require the same individualized attention necessary in every other aspect of ordeal ritual. Ordeal crisis often results in an extreme emotional outpouring, so bouts of tears, laughter, rage, or other emotions can be helpful clues. However, some seekers experience their crisis more strongly as cognitive dissonance, in which mental anguish may not produce crying or screaming or other obvious signs. Some seekers simply do not emote much, even when their crisis *is* deeply emotional, so facilitators must look for other signs that the seeker has found their obstacle.

Perhaps the most reliable indication that a seeker has reached crisis is the inadequacy of language. The seeker might attempt to explain what they've realized, but be unable to put it into words, or they might say something that sounds entirely normal as if it is the most profound statement they've ever spoken. Sometimes a seeker will speak their revelation, but then express dissatisfaction with the apparent simplicity of the words they chose. They might repeat old or familiar phrases, saying things like, "I knew it was true before, but I didn't really understand it until now." All of these are examples of the profound and unknowable power of ordeal. When the seeker has found something that cannot be easily encapsulated or explained, they have found the center of their ordeal.

Occasionally an ordeal will unravel revelation in a series of smaller crises, rather than erupt at a single point of epiphany. For example, a seeker undergoing an ordeal to confront her relationship with her body found that there was no single point at which she suddenly understood the answers to the questions she started with. Instead, there were several stages of the ordeal in which different pieces of her self-image snapped into focus. Each one came with its own emotional peak and followed its own course of integration. All of these revelations together overlapped and intertwined to create a sense of moving in and out of the crisis stage of her ordeal. Her experience stands as a reminder that while our categorized phases are useful for articulate discussion, reality is often more complex than out tidy templates, so we must remember *why* recognizing a point of crisis is significant in the first place.

When a seeker reaches their crisis, the facilitator must accept and support whatever that crisis happens to be for the seeker. A facilitator should challenge statements and assumptions made by the seeker during the approach stage, but not the inarticulable revelations discovered in crisis. Unintentionally projecting personal issues and assumptions onto a seeker is one of the major dangers in facilitating an ordeal ritual. This danger becomes more extreme the closer a seeker gets to crisis, and reaches its peak in that moment when the seeker finds their inner truth. A facilitator who challenges or casts doubt upon that truth can invalidate the seeker's journey. The facilitator's job is not to bring the seeker closer to who they as the facilitator think the seeker should be, but to help the seeker become the self they want for themselves. Accepting the crises, solutions, and revelations a seeker finds for themselves is essential to this process.

When a seeker discovers what "the real problem" is, or when they realize what they need to do, or when they suddenly understand what something means, accept their revelation. Whether you understand or agree with it or not, validate their experience, because it is they who are seeking, not you, and their answers will be different from yours. Support their process, however it takes shape, because it is this process of crisis and revelation that will yield the change that empowers them.

Do not assume that you have failed to facilitate an ordeal experience if the seeker does not seem to reach a climactic point of crisis. Revelations can unfold slowly, presenting more like a gradual crescendo than a crashing wave, and at times these types of crises are only obvious in retrospect. I once worked with a seeker who felt uncertain about whether or not her ritual brought her to ordeal until the following day. Her process had been a slow untangling of internal thoughts and feelings, and her revelation did not come as a single point of epiphany, but rather as small incremental insights. As we parted afterwards she felt satisfied with her ritual, but uncertain about whether or not it had brought the tremendous transformation she'd been seeking. When we checked in with each other the next day, she expressed a feeling of lightness and joy, and realized that her process had been so subtle that she hadn't seen how much it had transformed her until she could stand on the other side looking back at the beginning.

However your seeker's crisis takes shape, follow them along their path. Just as their expectations can spoil them for other opportunities, so can your expectations as the facilitator cause you to lead someone astray. If their revelation hits them in an inarticulable moment, validate their epiphany. If they tiptoe toward a new self over the course of several hours, match their pace and work with their process. Remember that your job is not to choose the seeker's path for them, but rather to shed just enough light on their darkness that they can find their own way through.

Chapter 19: Change

Once a seeker reaches the crisis of their ordeal, they must resolve that conflict through some form of change. Sometimes this crisis and change manifest together in the form of a revelation. A new understanding of something inevitably changes how we engage with it, especially when that thing is ourselves. These revelations can come suddenly—a crash of insight that changes everything—or they can come gradually, a slowly unfolding understanding of complexity and nuance that was previously unreachable. In both of these situations, crisis and change are intertwined. We could say that the crisis is the recognition that the old understanding was inaccurate or inadequate, and the change is the new understanding that replaces the old one, but our experience of that transformation is not a two-step process. Rather, recognition of the need for a new understanding, and that new understanding itself, come as a single revelation.

Other ordeals offer crisis and change as distinct stages of the ritual process. This is more common when the source of a seeker's internal conflict is particularly unexpected. For example, I once worked with a seeker who wanted to challenge their sense of gender during an ordeal ritual. Before the ritual they expressed a strong desire to connect with their femininity, but an inability to reconcile that desire with other characteristics which they felt were masculine. The ritual plan included forced feminization combined with what the seeker felt were unfeminine activities. This combination was meant to challenge the understanding of gender they were struggling with, and we facilitators were ready to support whatever they decided feminine and masculine meant to them during the course of their ordeal. Once the ritual started, however, it became clear that we would need to abandon our plan entirely. Our interactions and discourse during the approach stage revealed that the source of the seeker's struggling was not preconceptions about what it meant to be feminine, but about what it meant to be masculine. Their crisis was recognizing that toxic masculinity had defined their understanding of what it was to be a man, and that their expressions of femininity felt uncomfortable because they were more about being not-masculine than they were about being feminine. The most physical portion of their ordeal ritual happened not in the approach phase, nor in the crisis phase, but in the change phase, where they had to act with masculinity, and in doing so create what they wanted masculinity to mean for them. With a newly forged positive understanding of masculinity, they could craft both masculine and feminine forms of self expression that were not based on those qualities being in opposition to one another, but were based in a personal understanding of what those qualities meant to them, and how both were worthy of celebration in their own right.

When crisis offers revelation, the change exists in that new perspective, and so crisis and change arrive together. One could argue that all ordeal crises offer revelation, so dividing crisis and change into separate categories is little more than semantics. In a purely conceptual sense this is true, but my purpose in looking at the different stages of ordeal ritual is to identify how we facilitators can best support seekers on their journey. During approach, the facilitator should challenge the seeker's assumptions and statements, urging them to examine everything they think they know about themselves and the world, because it is through this agonizing introspection that the seeker will identify their crisis. Once that crisis is found, however, the facilitator must accept whatever the seeker discovers, and whatever meaning they assign to that discovery. As soon as the seeker begins to change in response to that crisis, facilitators may shift their engagement toward more active support, going beyond mere acceptance and into encouragement.

If we continue our analogy of an ordeal ritual as a journey for which we've constructed a careful map, but during which we must explore uncharted territory, then the moment of crisis is when the seeker finds in the center of that unknown area a tree bearing an infinite variety of fruit. As the seeker examines the tree, we must not tell them which fruit to pick, because only they will know which is food, and which is poison. The stage of change begins when the seeker picks their fruit and begins to eat it. Now we facilitators must not cast judgment upon which fruit they chose, nor criticize how slowly or sloppily they eat it, but must accept and support their choice.

In the case of the seeker mentioned above, this meant that during the approach of their ordeal I would ruthlessly challenge every characteristic they assigned to masculinity or femininity. Their crisis involved recognizing that those definitions needed to change; I was careful to keep my opinions to myself as they closed in on that revelation, so that they could choose for themselves exactly what needed changing. Once they began to act on their revelation, I shifted my interactions to include explicit affirmations. I watched what they did and how they did it, pointing out the things they chose to express as positively masculine in a way that validated their experience and supported their choices.

This tangle of crisis and change comprises the unpredictable outcome of ordeal ritual, the unknowable solution at the core of the uncertainty that makes a challenging experience into an ordeal. The ambiguity, profundity, and uncertainty of these solutions make them exceedingly difficult to write about. They are by their very nature experiences that defy declarative knowledge, and thus buck the tidy words that attempt to describe them. At the same time, the inadequacy of words serves as the first indicator that you've reached these states of inarticulable transformation.

The change that begins in an ordeal ritual does not end when the ritual is over. Even in instances of striking revelation, change continues as you decide how that new understanding of your self and your world will impact your actions. Slower processes of building change also continue past the ritual's end. The seeker who crafted a new foundation for their experience of masculinity did not walk away from their ritual perfectly able to embrace all aspects of their gender identity. They must continue to build upon that foundation, examining their relationship with gender as they explore their sense of self, grow as an individual, and learn how to express themselves in ways that are healthy for them.

Facilitators and seekers both must accept that an ordeal ritual is not a comprehensive solution to life's problems. Facilitators cannot "fix" seekers, and seekers cannot stop changing when the ritual is over. In future chapters we will delve deeper into how seekers can best engage with what ordeal rituals have to offer. For now we must remember that the change stage in an ordeal ritual marks the beginning of a larger process, but does not contain its end.

Chapter 20: Recovery

Ordeal rituals bring the seeker to an altered state in which radical change is possible, and perhaps even inevitable. Before they can resume their everyday life, the seeker must return to their normal state of being, and this recovery process begins with aftercare. We have already discussed what aftercare might include in the chapter on Planning Aftercare, so once your seeker is ready for this stage, all you need to do is follow your aftercare plan. The tricky part is figuring out how and when to make that transition.

As you draw closer to the recovery stage, consider the resilience factors you inventoried before you began the ritual. Seekers with fewer resilience factors will usually benefit from more support as they transition from crisis through recovery. Devote more time and attention to the pacing of your transition when the seeker has fewer support structures to rely on outside of your ritual, and increase the likelihood that your seeker will positively integrate their experience by helping them find resources that will help them process it. Remember that you do not need to personally provide all of the support your seeker needs, and usually would not be able to provide it even if you were to try; you must help the seeker *find* that support, but do not necessarily need to *be* it.

All ordeals require individualized attention to figure out when the seeker is ready to transition to aftercare. The seeker may need some time to revel in what they've learned in crisis, or might need a rapid transition to emphasize an experience of insight or relief. First and foremost, use your communication plan to figure out what the seeker wants, and let that guide your decisions. This is not a time to question the seeker's desires; simply help them get what they need in order to integrate what they learned in their ordeal. That integration begins with validation, which in turn begins with respecting and responding to what they ask for.

A facilitator should always transition to aftercare immediately when a seeker calls for an end to their ordeal. It does not matter whether this end is a result of something gone wrong, or whether the seeker claimed authority over their limits in the change stage of their ordeal. If the ritual went awry, you show the seeker that you care for their well-being by giving them the support they asked for during your planning and negotiation. If the ordeal achieved its intended purpose, stopping when they call to stop validates their revelation about their limits. Either way, the best possible outcome requires affirming their agency by respecting their desire for an end, and immediately moving to aftercare.

In catharsis ordeals, the seeker usually needs time to fully release whatever they need to get rid of before they can begin their recovery. In these situations, the seeker often knows when they are ready to transition to aftercare. They will feel lighter, emotionally relieved, and ready to move forward. When catharsis is a possibility in an ordeal ritual, include in your communication plan some way of checking in with the seeker to find out when they are ready for that shift to aftercare. Some seekers will feel perfectly comfortable with you simply asking if they are ready, but others will want time to sit with their experience without needing to articulate anything. Remember that nonverbal cues are an excellent option for these types of situations.

Great care is necessary when an ordeal makes an attempt at catharsis, but the seeker never gets any lighter despite an outpouring of emotion. In such a situation the seeker may not be ready to let go of their feelings about the source of their emotional pain, especially when that source involves some form of trauma. Sometimes people need to remember and mourn their experience before they can be ready to work through it. Allowing some time for the seeker to express their feelings can be constructive for their long term well-being, but dwelling in that agony can be unhealthy. Let the seeker have time to feel what they feel, and then firmly but gently remind them that what happened in the past is past. Call their attention back to the present through simple acts of bodily awareness. Slow, deep, intentional breaths are an excellent way to accomplish this. Reassure the seeker that being unable to let go of their feelings does not mean they have "failed" their ordeal; mourning is a necessary part of the overall healing process, and understanding where they are in that process is a valuable insight. Encourage the seeker to continue this process with their therapist if they have one, or with other support figures in their life if they do not.

Aftercare begins a process of reflection and integration that will last long after the ordeal ritual comes to an end. Your communication plan included post-ritual communication for exactly this reason. Do not push yourself or your seeker to articulate your experience during ritual aftercare if that doesn't feel right to *both* of you. Allow yourselves time to sit with the inarticulately profound nature of ordeal if that is what you need. Remember that if either one of you needs to express something before the other is ready to hear it, you can write that thing down, and then save what you wrote for whenever the other party is able to begin a dialogue. It is possible to allow for time and space alone without causing anyone else to feel that their voice must be silenced. Everyone participating in an ordeal ritual should be ready to practice patience and compassion during the time that follows it.

Integrating an ordeal experience takes time because the seeker must learn how their revelation applies to their life. Sometimes this seems very simple, but just as knowing change and understanding change are completely different, so too are understanding change and living change. Ordeal ritual is not a quick "fix" or "cure", but rather a tool for long term personal growth and empowerment. The ritual does not end personal work; it facilitates that work, helping the seeker see what work needs to be done, and offering insight about how to do it. When the ritual is over, that work still needs doing. As your seeker processes their ordeal, remind them of all the resilience factors you inventoried during your initial negotiation. Help them know where they can continue to seek help and find support in figuring out how they want to act upon what they discovered in their ordeal. Also remember that you too will need to process your experience as the facilitator. Remember your own support structures, and use them.

Part IV
Seeking Change

Chapter 21: The Seeker's Role

Until now, our examination of ordeal has focused primarily on the facilitator's point of view. With all the planning and preparing required to create an ordeal ritual, the facilitator's role is more firmly rooted in the declarative, and thus easier to write about. Nevertheless, the seeker must take an active role in uncovering their power and seizing transformation. While this internal process is more difficult to articulate, it still warrants examination. In this section we will take a closer look at how seekers can establish an intent that will create context for their ordeal ritual, what they might want to consider while choosing a facilitator or facilitating team, and how to seek change in their moment of crisis.

Just as the facilitator's point of view is also relevant to seekers, so is the seeker's point of view relevant to facilitators. No matter how you plan to (or happen to) engage in ordeal, understanding the perspective of all participants helps create a better experience for everyone. If you are reading this book solely to learn how to be a better facilitator, then as you read about the seeker's process, consider how your approach impacts their experience, and what you might adjust to better facilitate their journey.

Chapter 22: Crafting Intent

A planned ordeal ritual begins with an intent: what do you want the ritual to do? This intent is going to be the foundation for your mindset, so how you articulate that intent is almost as important as the intent itself. The ways in which we talk about things, even if only to ourselves, impacts how we think about them. For example, I chose to name this chapter "Crafting Intent" because the word "crafting" brings to mind an active process: something we must work to create, rather than something we simply find or uncover. Crafting your intent is as much about figuring out what you want to challenge in your ordeal ritual as it is about figuring out how to articulate that challenge, both to yourself and to your facilitator.

Begin by asking yourself a question that is far more complex than it first appears: What's really bothering you? Talk to a friend or partner about your struggle, or write it down if you'd prefer to keep this part of your process private. Note your first response, acknowledge it, and then ask yourself *why* that thing bothers you. Heap those "whys" upon yourself like a four-year-old questioning authority.

You might find that your "whys" end with an "I don't know." In some cases, this point can be reached rather rapidly. For example, if I wanted an ordeal ritual designed around my fear of spiders, asking myself why I'm afraid of them would immediately end with "I don't know." I cannot remember any traumatic experience involving a spider, and as far as I know I've been terrified of them for my entire life. That first "why" leaves me immediately ready to go on to the next stage in crafting my intent.

If, on the other hand, I wanted an ordeal ritual designed around my negative feelings about my appearance, I could talk or write for hours about why I have such harsh opinions about my own body. Between stories about how I was raised, being bullied in school, and facing prejudice as an overweight adult, I could talk or write for hours about why I agonize about my shape at a size 10 just as much as I did at a size 24. These rational explanations could go on endlessly in a tangle of personal experience and societal expectations, none of which would actually help me find the change I want. I will know that I am ready for the next stage in crafting my intent when the same issue comes up again and again, when my rationale either feels hollow or is discordant with my emotions, or when my logic begins to circle through the same thoughts over and over. In my example, it ends up looking a bit like this:

I am afraid of being overweight because our society treats large people very poorly. I do not want our society to treat large people poorly. Towards that end, I should embrace my body in whatever shape it has, rather than bowing to social pressure, because when I bow to social pressure I become part of the problem. It is a real problem, though—our society does treat large people poorly, and I am afraid of being overweight because our society treats large people poorly...

I could cycle in this combination of self and cultural analysis for hours, but once I reach that looped logic, the exercise of internal reflection has been as useful as it's going to be. At that point I must find the piece within the circle that is worth drawing out and facing in an ordeal ritual. Often this is extremely difficult for us to find for ourselves. Friends, partners, and facilitators can all help us see what we are talking around rather than saying outright, or they can point out the metaphorical elephant in the room.

In my case, the issue I'm avoiding is that it's not size itself I fear, but how people treat me because of my appearance. From there the question becomes simpler, and also harder: leaving physical dimensions out of it entirely, if people do treat me poorly based on my appearance, then what? How do I want to handle it? How do I want to respond? At last, my answer here is that I don't know. In a vague sense I can say that I want to react with confidence and courage, and that I want my response to convey and create the body-positivity I want to exist in the world. Ultimately, however, I have no idea how to do that, or what that kind of response would look like for me.

The most critical piece in this process is developing an awareness of the unknown. We must acknowledge that there are elements of ourselves we do not understand in order to avoid the type of expectation that will lead to failure. This means admitting that we do not have all the answers. Acknowledging that we don't know it all creates space for revelation in ordeal.

Since we must not engage with our personal unknowns with an expectation of what they will teach us, we must instead conceptualize our ordeal ritual intent as an approach to that unknown region. We know the general area of our ourselves that we want to explore, but how do we get there? We craft this approach within our minds by phrasing our intent in open-ended statements.

Let us consider both of the examples above. First, consider the ordeal ritual designed around a fear of spiders. An intent loaded with expectation would sound something like this: *"My intent is to conquer my fear of spiders."*

This goal allows for only one possible solution to the ordeal: fearlessness. While I have, in fact, overcome a fear during an ordeal ritual before, this type of outcome is unlikely in the case of true phobias. I probably won't be able to shake off my fear of spiders during the course of a single ritual, so creating an expectation of that outcome sets me up for failure, and pressures me to look solely in that direction for a successful experience. If I were instead to find some better way of *managing* my fear, I might not recognize that as a worthwhile revelation if I am too focused on *overcoming* my fear.

Here's a better way for me to phrase my intent: *"My intent is to confront my fear of spiders."*

This goal allows for any and all types of revelations gained through that confrontation to be celebrated as a productive outcome. Were I to overcome my fear somehow, then fearlessness would be the outcome of that confrontation. However, if I were to find a better coping mechanism, but still end the ordeal just as fearful as I started, I will still have gained something of value from that confrontation, and my ordeal ritual can still be considered a success.

The more complex the issue we want to face in ordeal, the more difficult it can be to figure out how to craft a statement of intent with adequately open-ended phrasing. In the example of my body-image issues, there are several ways I could articulate my intent, both with and without expectation:

- With expectation: "I want to be happier with my body."
- Without expectation: "I want to confront my feelings about my body."
- With expectation: "I don't want to care how people treat me based on my looks."
- Without expectation: "I want to face my fear that people will treat me poorly based on my looks."
- With expectation: "I want to be more body-positive."
- Without expectation: "I want to find out what body-positivity means to me."

In general, an expectation states what you want to learn, whereas an intent without expectation states what you want to learn *from*. My statements with expectation outline a specific outcome: be happier about my body, stop caring what people think, be body-positive. For all that these sound like positive messages, phrasing my intent in these ways is tremendously limiting, and potentially damaging if it causes me to ignore or resist some other form of positive change. My statements without expectation each offer an approach to insight: confront my feelings, face my fear, find out what body positivity means to me. Because those statements do not mandate what I should learn from my experience, any insight I gain can be an answer to my intent.

Once I choose a facilitator for my ordeal ritual, I will share with them all of these statements of intent as different facets of a single core issue. My facilitator might choose one of those statements to focus on, or they might create a ritual that touches on all of them. Either way, the full context of what I am wrestling with and what I want to get out of it will be helpful to both of us.

Chapter 23: Choosing a Facilitator

The expectations we must so carefully avoid in ordeal work are expectations about our outcome; we must enter ordeal open to whatever we might learn in our suffering. This is not to say that all expectations are fundamentally unhealthy. As a seeker, you should absolutely expect your facilitator to respect your limits. Ordeal is not an excuse for any form of assault or consent violation. While we must carefully remove expectation from our intent, we must just as carefully examine and communicate our expectations of our facilitators.

This process begins with understanding our own personal definition of "ordeal". The concept of ordeal put forth in this book constitutes my personal philosophy, and describes how I approach various forms of ordeal work. This is by no means a universal definition. As you begin searching for a facilitator for your ordeal ritual, you should articulate in your own mind what the word "ordeal" means to you. Make sure that whatever facilitator you choose understands your definition, and that you understand theirs. Your definitions do not need to match exactly, but you must both understand what you hope to accomplish through the experience you create, and what are the various responsibilities of everyone involved. Consider asking yourself the following questions before you interview a potential facilitator:

- ❖ What makes an experience into an ordeal for me?
- ❖ What is my favorite metaphor for ordeal?
- ❖ How much guidance do I want my facilitator to offer during my ordeal?
- ❖ How much interaction do I want with my facilitator before my ordeal?
- ❖ How much interaction do I want with my facilitator after my ordeal?
- ❖ How much control do I want over the details of my ordeal ritual? Would this depend on how well I know my facilitator?
- ❖ How much disclosure do I need about the details of my ordeal ritual? Would this depend on how well I know my facilitator?

- ❖ Would I prefer to work with someone I know, or with someone new?
- ❖ Is this a personal issue I only want to reveal to someone I know well enough to trust with it?
- ❖ Do I want a facilitator who doesn't have a personal bias about me or my issue?

There are no wrong answers to any of these questions. Ordeal is deeply personal work, and thus is bound to look different for each individual. The point of this process is not to bring yourself closer to any specific definition of ordeal, but to understand what ordeal means to you. Once you know what kind of ordeal experience you want, you will be better able to communicate those wants to potential facilitators, and evaluate whether or not their definitions are compatible with yours.

Finding a potential facilitator to interview is not an easy task. Start by asking people you know if they have any suggestions, especially if you are already part of a community where at least some people are likely to have heard of the concept. If you're not, consider reaching out through social media or online forums, but do so with a healthy dose of discernment. The world is full of people who seem to be credible facilitators, but have little awareness or understanding of what they're actually doing. Ask for references, both from people who taught that facilitator how to do what they do, and from that facilitator's former seekers.

One of the biggest dangers to avoid in any facilitator is ego. A good facilitator must be able to admit that they are fallible, take accountability for their actions, and learn from their mistakes. While it is important to negotiate how you would resolve potential conflicts or respond to accidents, even astoundingly egotistical facilitators can handle these negotiations with apparent humility. Furthermore, it can be difficult to tell the difference between a facilitator who is confident in their skills and a facilitator who is dangerously arrogant.

The best way I've found to test this is to ask the facilitator to refer me to someone else. This method is not foolproof. Just because a facilitator can provide referrals does not automatically mean they are safe to work with. Sometimes a facilitator will happily give referrals because it feeds their ego to show how many other facilitators they know.

On the other hand, if a potential facilitator insists that they alone are able to provide the experience you need, they are almost certainly dangerous. Even if their technical skills are excellent, personal investment in the facilitating role leads to a mindset that causes facilitators to push where *they* think a seeker needs to go, rather than urging a seeker along on their own journey. A good facilitator will be able to suggest other individuals who could facilitate the ordeal, or at the very least offer other people to talk to who might have suggestions for other facilitators. This is often the case when an ordeal ritual requires specialized skills, such as psychology training to support a trauma victim, or specific techniques for physical experiences. Sometimes finding an individual with the right combination of skills is quite difficult. The best a potential facilitator might be able to offer is someone who has other contacts or suggestions, even if that person couldn't facilitate the ordeal themselves. A good potential facilitator will offer support in finding other options, rather than putting forth themselves as the only possible solution.

When you've found someone you think might be a good match for you and your ordeal, dive deeper into communication and negotiation. Use the chapters you've read thus far to help you articulate what you want, and what you don't want. Expect your facilitator to respect your needs and limits, and respect theirs in turn.

As you negotiate with your facilitator, let your personal approach to ordeal influence what questions you ask and what information you disclose. You are not required to share anything you don't want to share, but consider what might constitute informed consent for both yourself and your facilitator. Aim your discussion at creating that informed consent for everyone involved. If your facilitator asks a question you don't want to answer, it is better to tell them that you don't want to answer it, rather than giving the answer you think they want to hear, or making up an answer. It's always alright to ask why they want a certain piece of information, and if the reason they give is unsatisfactory, you can decline to give it.

Consider sharing the following information with your facilitator:

- ❖ What ordeal means to you
- ❖ What spiritual context, if any, ordeal has for you
- ❖ Your intent for this ordeal ritual
- ❖ Medical issues, allergies, and other physical concerns
- ❖ Mental health concerns and relevant care procedures
- ❖ Mental and physical triggers
- ❖ Medications and potential side effects
- ❖ Effective coping mechanisms and deescalation techniques
- ❖ Aftercare needs
- ❖ Hard limits
- ❖ Soft limits

Consider asking your facilitator the following questions:

- ❖ What does ordeal mean to you?
- ❖ Is ordeal sacred or spiritual to you? If so, what does that mean?
- ❖ How would you approach my intent?
- ❖ Who else might be able to facilitate for me?
- ❖ What are your strongest skills?
- ❖ What are your weakest skills?
- ❖ Who can vouch for your skills?
- ❖ How did you learn to facilitate ordeals?

Consider answering the following questions collaboratively with your facilitator:

- ❖ How frequently do you want to communicate before the ritual, and through which media?
- ❖ When do you want to do this ritual?
- ❖ When are you available to do this ritual?
- ❖ Where do you want to do this ritual?
- ❖ How far are you willing to travel for this ritual?
- ❖ Do you have a venue in mind?
- ❖ Could you host the ritual on your property?

- ❖ Do you want the ritual to work within a specific spiritual, magical, or religious system or paradigm?
- ❖ Do you want a single facilitator or a team of facilitators?
- ❖ Do you want witnesses?
- ❖ How will we communicate during the ordeal?
- ❖ Who will provide aftercare for whom?
- ❖ How would you want to respond to an accident or mistake?
- ❖ How would you want to resolve conflict if something goes wrong?
- ❖ How frequently do you want to communicate after the ritual, and through which media?
- ❖ Who could serve as an intermediary if we don't want to communicate directly after the ordeal?

These lists are meant to serve as a starting point for a larger conversation. They are not comprehensive checklists. The chapters on Safer Seeking through Planning Aftercare more thoroughly investigate negotiation for ordeal rituals, and are relevant to both seekers and facilitators. Understanding what questions a potential facilitator should ask will help you prepare your responses as a seeker. Furthermore, understanding why those questions are significant can help you evaluate whether or not you want to work with that facilitator. Familiarity with the process will leave you more ready to participate in it, and also better able to figure out who isn't asking the right questions.

If a negotiation process with a facilitator makes you feel uncomfortable, you can always change your mind about working with that facilitator. It is never too late to back out. In fact, the negotiation process exists not only to establish healthy parameters for your ordeal ritual, but also to build rapport between yourself and your facilitator. If that rapport is unhealthy or unsatisfying, then your ritual is at risk for similar results. Sometimes clarification can ease those communication issues, especially when the problem is related to a specific media. For example, if you've only been communicating with your facilitator through email and it just doesn't seem to be going well, consider a phone call or a face-to-face meeting before you call it quits. That said, if you simply don't get along, or feel uncomfortable with your facilitator, it's better to walk away than to proceed despite misgivings.

Your ordeal ritual facilitator might ask that you compensate them for their work, especially when the materials required for the ritual are expensive. The subject of payment for ordeal facilitation is deeply sensitive for some, and generally very personal, so make sure to ask a potential facilitator how they feel about compensation, and what, if anything, they might want in return. Even if your ritual is being facilitated by a friend or loved one who is unlikely to ask for anything in exchange, making the offer is still a lovely way to show appreciation for their work.

My personal feelings on this subject are neatly summarized by the concept of fair and equitable exchange: when discussing an ordeal ritual, whether I'm the seeker or the facilitator, I talk to the other person or people about what effort and resources are being put into the ritual, taking into account design, materials, travel, preparation, and execution. Then together we decide what constitutes a fair exchange, with trade options including money, items, and services. The compensation I've most frequently received as a facilitator is a home-cooked meal; preparing food that accommodates my various dietary restrictions is a skill I do not possess and highly value, so I find such a trade to be deeply satisfying. The point here is not to feed the ego of a facilitator by paying them outrageous sums of money, nor is it to restrict access to ordeal ritual by making it available only to the wealthy. The point is to express appreciation and convey value through whatever exchange feels appropriate to everyone involved.

Chapter 24: The Art of Becoming

Seeking empowerment through ordeal is an act that sounds very simple on paper but is exquisitely challenging in practice: be confident in your ability to succeed, be open to any possible definition of success, and discover who you want to become. Of course, finding that confidence and openness is harder than it sounds, even for the most naturally confident and open among us. Ordeal takes us into the most conflicted areas of ourselves, and necessarily shakes our beliefs so that we can see where our metaphorical structures are unsound. We must be willing to recognize where change is crucial and know how to find the strength to create it. We must know how to find our resilience.

Internal resilience factors are attributes that make you as a seeker more likely to constructively integrate your ordeal experience. Even when these attributes are not naturally part of your personality, you can begin to create a resilient mindset for yourself by intentionally shifting the way you think about an upcoming ordeal ritual. Take some time to meditate or reflect during the days leading up to your ritual, and consider using the following statements to focus your thoughts:

- ❖ I can do this.
- ❖ I can ask for help if I need it.
- ❖ I will learn something useful from this ritual.
- ❖ It's OK that I don't know how it will end.
- ❖ I'm not supposed to have all the answers.
- ❖ I can decide what my experience means to me.
- ❖ I want to learn what changes I need.
- ❖ I am ready to change.

Communication will be critical during your processing period after the ordeal. If you normally struggle to share your thoughts and feelings, get some practice in before the ordeal starts. Talk to friends or loved ones about your intent for the ritual, and share how you think and feel about it. Keep a journal in the days or weeks leading up to the ordeal, and re-read old entries to get some perspective on how you communicate with yourself.

Coping skills can be a tremendous source of strength in an ordeal ritual, even when you don't end up using them. We are more willing to endure when we know that comfort awaits us on the other side of suffering. Think about what has helped you feel better after difficult experiences in the past. Do you need time to cuddle with your dog? Is there a comfort food that helps you feel better? Does a favorite TV show help you shake off stress? Make a list of everything that has helped you before, then go over your list and decide which items might be useful and practical resources to help you recover from your ordeal.

External resilience factors are elements of your environment that will help you constructively process your ordeal. In the time leading up to your ritual, make a list of all the resources you have available to support your processing. The questions posed below will help you come up with your list, but remember that the point is not to claim as many items as you can, but just to recognize what support structures you have. We all live very different lives, and intentional ordeal ritual is for everyone, not just the wealthy or the privileged. If there's something on the list you don't have, remember that is perfectly normal, and move on. Focus on what support structures you do have, not on what you don't.

- ❖ Who are my mentors or positive role models?
- ❖ Who is willing to support me through my ordeal process?
- ❖ Who will support me in a more general sense, even if I can't talk to them about my ritual?
- ❖ Which peer or social groups will support me through my ordeal process?
- ❖ Which peer or social groups will support me in a more general sense, even if I can't talk to them about my ritual?
- ❖ How do I care for my health?
- ❖ Who helps me care for my health?
- ❖ Am I financially stable?
- ❖ Is my living environment secure?
- ❖ What do I do for fun?
- ❖ Do I like my job?
- ❖ Do I enjoy my work environment?

❖ Do I see a therapist or other mental health professional?

In an ideal world, we are all easily able to talk to our therapists about whatever issues we struggle with. Our world, however, is far from ideal, and finding a therapist with whom one can speak frankly about subjects like ordeal ritual is extremely difficult. The best place to start searching for one would be the National Coalition for Sexual Freedom's a publicly available database of BDSM-friendly healthcare professionals. So long as your ritual includes informed and mutually consenting adults, a kink-aware therapist is likely to understand and be able to support your process.

If you can't find a kink-friendly therapist, or if you already have a therapist you like but for any reason don't feel comfortable sharing the details of an ordeal ritual with them, it is still possible to seek their support in processing your ordeal experience. In the aftermath of an ordeal ritual, what matters most is what that experience meant to you, and what you want to do with what you learned. Lying to your therapist will not help either of you, but you can honestly tell them what's been on your mind, and simply omit what you don't want to share. Talking about your thoughts and feelings following the ritual can allow them to help you with your processing without needing to get into the details of what happened.

Figuring out how to have that type of conversation can be difficult, but is usually worth it. Think about what you learned in your ordeal, and what impact it has on greater themes in your life. For example, a woman who underwent a relief ordeal in which she was shamed and humiliated by her facilitators did not feel that there was any way her therapist could understand it as a constructive experience. As she reflected on the ritual, she focused on what she learned about herself, and how that information might be both useful and challenging. The humiliation was a relief to her because her internal criticism could rest while that pattern was held by someone else, but it did not achieve the desired catharsis because she could not give up or get rid of that pattern within her own mind. She had not realized until then just how critical she was of herself, and wanted to work towards changing that. When she next saw her therapist, she sought help by focusing on what she had learned, and on what she wanted: "I think I'm too hard on myself, but I don't know what to do about it." Her therapist then carried this work forward, supporting her as she continued the process catalyzed by the ritual.

Sometimes a therapist will pointedly ask why a particular subject is coming up, or what happened that made you want to talk about this now. If that happens to you, and you don't want to talk about your ritual, honesty is still the best policy. If you don't want to talk about it, tell them you don't want to talk about it. Personal boundaries are, after all, perfectly healthy, and your therapist ought to respect yours. You can still seek their help by saying that you'd rather focus on how those thoughts and feelings might impact the future, rather than reflecting on past scenarios.

If you have a therapist you trust, and with whom you feel very comfortable, you might want to attempt educating your therapist about ordeal ritual. More and more frequently I hear about people whose therapists were open to learning about subjects that were entirely new to them in the interest of helping their client. If you suspect this might be the case, broach the subject *before* your ritual rather than after. It is absolutely wonderful that so many therapists are now open to learning about different ways of thinking, believing, living, and loving. Nevertheless, educating a therapist about your lifestyle, beliefs, or identity can be very tiring. It is most certainly worthwhile work, but it is *work* nonetheless, and attempting to do that work while also processing an ordeal experience will make everything harder on you. Talk to your therapist ahead of time about what ordeal means to you, and figure out how much of your experience you will feel comfortable sharing. That way, when it comes time to process your ritual, you will already know how you want talk about it with your therapist, and can focus on working through what you learned rather than working out how they can help.

As your ordeal ritual draws closer, resist the urge to over-prepare. Ready yourself by reflecting on the inner conflict you want to address in your ritual, let your intent guide you, and be ready for unexpected insight. Remind yourself that you have no idea what it's going to be like, and that's a good thing. Prime your mind to be receptive to unpredictable insights.

The most essential requirement for a seeker is ruthless authenticity. Ordeal requires confronting uncomfortable truths. If authenticity means living as who you truly are, ruthless authenticity means accepting the ugly truths right alongside the beautiful ones. Venture into ordeal willing to see the parts of yourself you'd rather not acknowledge. Accept that before you can become a self you want to be, you must recognize the ways in which what you are isn't what you want.

Acknowledging what we don't like about ourselves does not mean that we are entirely bad, unhealthy, or unworthy. It means we have grown enough as individuals to be ready for improvement. Perhaps we have changed and didn't realize it, or perhaps something that was once good for us no longer serves, or perhaps we are only now capable of confronting that dark corner of the soul we left untouched for so many years. Whatever the reason for it, accept that change is normal, healthy, and necessary.

Finally, remember that you can always stop your ritual if you need to. If something starts to go wrong, tell your facilitator as soon as possible. Use the communication plan you came up with, and convey to the best of your ability what you're feeling, what you're thinking, and what you need. Your facilitator will be doing their best to look for clues and cues that will show the way to your intent, but they are not perfect, and cannot read your mind. The more you share with them about your state of being, the better they will be able to reflect that back to you, and the better you will be able to see what you need to see. Allow them the opportunity to adjust if you need a different approach, more support, or just a moment to pause and catch your breath before you continue.

The difference between what is uncomfortable but necessary and what is uncomfortable and unhealthy can be difficult to discern in the heat of the moment. We often cannot see how a miserable experience will lead to constructive results until after the misery has passed. There is, however, one sure way to determine if your ordeal should continue or not: consent. *Do you want to continue? If so, then do. If you don't, then don't.* You need no greater reason to stop than that you want to.

On a few rare occasions, I have asked someone I trust to push me farther than I would want to go on my own. Two key factors made these experiences healthy for me. First, I knew that if I changed my mind and wanted to stop after all, my facilitator would stop. I knew how to communicate that to them, and had absolute confidence that they would respect my need to end the ordeal. Second, I internally reminded myself as I struggled through the experience that I chose to be pushed. I told myself again and again that I wanted this, that I asked for it, that it was my choice. Internally reaffirming my agency in this way gave me the resilience I needed to get through the ordeal. Combining these two factors meant that I also reminded myself that I could choose to end the ordeal if I wanted to, and every time I did not call for an end, I actively chose to let my facilitator push me farther. This engagement in the continuation of my ritual added to my resilience, and helped me see my own strength.

Let us be extremely clear, however, that what I am describing here is my own internal process for engaging with an ordeal in which my limits are consensually pushed. Just because someone exhibits the same external responses does not mean they are engaged in the same internal process. Facilitators must use their agreed-upon communication plan to continually establish mutual consent. I share my experience here not for facilitators, but for seekers. This is one example of how a seeker can internally engage with their ordeal process. It's a tool offered for use, not a standard for others to be judged against.

Chapter 25: Avoiding Ritual Dependence

Throughout this book we've talked about seeking solutions in ordeal ritual: the seeker identifies some inner conflict to approach, and then through ordeal discovers how to resolve that conflict. We must keep in mind, however, that the solutions we find in ordeal are not the sort that instantly fix all of your life. Each solution is like a puzzle piece, and once you get that piece you have to figure out how it fits into the whole of your life. Your puzzle is infinite, so you will always be able to find more pieces, but once you find them you must do the work of fitting the pieces together. That work happens outside of ritual space, in your everyday life.

If you just go through ordeal ritual after ordeal ritual without doing any of the work between, you won't end up with a coherent picture of yourself. What you'll have is a big pile of puzzle pieces, a knowledge that they fit together somehow, and maybe a vague sense of what picture they're going to make, but no true understanding of what that picture looks like because you haven't seen it yet. There is no photo on the puzzle box of life. The bigger your pile of pieces gets, the more overwhelming it will seem, and the longer it will take to fit all of them together.

Sometimes figuring out how a new insight fits into your life can be challenging, and it's possible to mistake this sense of challenge for a need to attempt another ordeal ritual. Such a ritual may well yield more insights, but it won't help you understand how to integrate what you've learned. There is no ordeal to show you how your puzzle pieces fit together. Real-life application can only be found in real life.

After an ordeal ritual, take time to figure out how you want your revelation to shape who you become. Put your ideas into practice and live the solution you found for yourself. When you think you've got a solid sense of what that ritual meant and how it has helped you grow, reflect on that process. Take a moment to look at your puzzle-in-progress, and see what you've got so far. You don't have to have *all* the pieces together before you reach for another; some of them might fit to a part of the puzzle you haven't gotten to yet, and that's OK. Just make sure that you've put together as many as you can, and that you don't have a huge pile waiting to be sorted through.

When you have a reliable way to find another puzzle piece, even if that way is difficult, it can seem easier to just reach for piece after piece rather than taking on the arduous task of putting them together. It can feel like you're making progress, because you have so many pieces, and isn't that something? But remember to keep an eye on the whole puzzle, and not focus only on the pieces. No matter how many pieces you get, if you never fit any of them in the puzzle, then little will have really changed.

I lean heavily upon metaphor here because the real process of integrating ordeal insights will be unique for each individual. I have been asked many times how long one should wait before attempting another ordeal, and there simply isn't a universal answer to that question. Sometimes people can be ready in weeks, whereas other people might need months or years. Some rituals are be designed to work in a series, with each one building upon the revelations gained in those that came before, so all must be processed together as a group when the full course is complete. Some ordeals are singular experiences, something that one never entirely finishes processing, but rather revisits again and again, gaining new insight as life offers new perspective.

Ultimately the best way to gauge whether or not you're ready for another ordeal ritual is to ask whether or not you're ready for the work that comes after. If you are still trying to figure out what your last ritual means for your life, do you have the mental, emotional, and physical resources to struggle through integrating another radical insight? Maybe another insight will help that struggle, but what if it doesn't? What if the revelation you find in your next ordeal requires work in an entirely different chapter of who you are? Will you be able to manage processing both? Make sure you ask yourself these questions, and be ruthlessly honest with your answers. Whatever you decide to do, remembering that your action was your choice will help you grow through your decision.

Part V
The Ordeal Path

Chapter 26: Living Ordeal

What does it mean to walk the ordeal path? This is a question I asked myself over and over as I studied, practiced, and sought my own revelations in ordeal ritual. How does the power of dissonance transform my life? Who do I become in my darkest moments? Who do I want to be, and how do I make those changes outside of ritual space?

Ordeal ritual is a powerful tool. We may choose to wield it or not, and consent is at the very core of its ethics and efficacy. Unexpected ordeal in a BDSM scene is—or at the very least should be—similar, in that consent is key, there's always a way out, and once we encounter ordeal, we may choose to engage or not. In fact, because so much of how people engage in BDSM is, in essence, ritual behavior, the tools put forth in this book for engaging with ordeal ritual can also be effective in handling unplanned ordeal experiences that arise spontaneously during kink scenes.

Ordeal as a way of life is different from scenes and rituals in that we often can't stop, avoid, or prevent what's causing our suffering. We can choose whether or not we wish to engage with that suffering as an ordeal, but we can't safeword out of chronic illness, getting laid off, or grieving a death. We can use concepts from ordeal ritual to help us engage with difficult or traumatic life events in a constructive way, but those concepts will only serve us well if we also respect how life events are different from the carefully constructed environment of an intentional ritual.

Dealing with painful life experiences is not something our society handles very well. As I observed how others responded to my suffering, and to the suffering of people around me, I noticed an overwhelming tendency to minimize, cover up, or outright ignore physical or emotional pain. Even in those who recognized suffering, there seemed to be a tremendous need to immediately make it better. Precious few were able to simply validate another's pain, and so perhaps it ought not be surprising that we so often struggle with accepting our own pain. In order to walk the ordeal path with respect, both to ourselves and to others, we need to change the ways in which we engage with suffering.

As you contemplate your own path, keep in mind that ordeal as a way of life is not about seeking constant suffering, nor does it imply that every life experience you have is an ordeal. The ordeal path is about seeking personal growth in those moments when you *must* suffer. By all means, seek joy, but when agony is unavoidable, you might as well learn from it.

Before we proceed, it's worth noting that ordeal ritual can serve as excellent practice for life ordeals. If you've learned how your own mind engages with suffering, what can boost your resilience, and how you best process your experiences, all of those skills will carry into handling life ordeals. While ordeal rituals and the ordeal path are different in significant ways, there are still many transferable skills between them.

Chapter 27: Value in Suffering

We grow through ordeal because it hurts. We cannot seek empowerment through ordeal by minimizing, dismissing, or ignoring that hurt, because the hurt itself is the source of empowerment. The very definition of ordeal requires suffering, and what we learn about ourselves arises from how we engage with that suffering. Thus, ordeal is not and *cannot be* about looking for the proverbial silver lining in every cloud. It's not "a good thing" that you suffered. Ordeal experiences are valuable because they were *not* good.

This was one of the many lessons I learned from my father's passing. My childhood was difficult, and my relationship with my mother was strained at best, but I adored my father. He was the buffer that kept my family from exploding, and he accepted me in ways that no other adult did. Losing him meant losing the only person in my family who really knew me, save my sister, and we lost him together.

The year that followed his death taught me more about myself than any other experience I'd ever had. Up until then, divorce had been my benchmark for emotional pain. I sat sobbing on the airplane back to the United States from Europe, where I'd lived with my ex-husband. I agonized over my decision to choose my own happiness rather than shape myself into the person my ex wanted me to be, and decided that I'd rather be selfish and true to myself than live the rest of my life as an illusion of a person. In the months that followed, I told myself that all of this was for the best. Leaving had hurt, but that was OK because it was a good thing I'd left. My life improved dramatically following my divorce, so it was easy to look around and see all the good I'd accomplished by leaving, and interpret that good as the value of my suffering.

When my father died two and a half years later, that logic shattered. Once more I learned about myself through emotional pain, but the price was too high. Nothing anyone could—or can—say would convince me that his death was worth what I learned, or that it was a good thing that he died. The mere thought of that is insulting. Nevertheless, I *did* learn, and I struggled with guilt over how much I changed for the better because of his death.

Understanding came gradually through mourning. As I grieved, I acknowledged that grief as the measure of my affection for him. I hurt because I loved him. In the beginning, that grief was too much to engage with directly. I barely left my apartment. He passed on the first of July, and I was an academic year teacher at the time, so I spent the summer lost in grief. I played computer games to escape during the day, staying up as late as I could in the hope that I would fall asleep quickly at night. I never did; flashbacks of touching his empty body the morning he died gripped me as soon as I closed my eyes. I would sob until exhaustion finally took me into sleep.

Things started to change with the school year. Work forced me to be out in the world again, and I found that I was more capable of living than I'd thought. I began to support my mother and sister in handling my father's affairs, and managed my own end of things independently. I discovered all the ways in which my father had sheltered us, and learned how to stand on my own and take care of myself. In some ways I finally grew up.

I liked who I was growing into. I was proud of how competent I'd become, and pleased with my independence. I also still hurt. My grief didn't disappear because I'd found some things to be happy about. I discovered that I could live, grow, and become a better person through losing my father, and still suffer his loss. These two things—suffering grief and happy growth—did not cancel each other out. One emerged not just from the other, but *because of* the other. I had changed so much precisely because losing him hurt so terribly. Anything less monumentally terrible would not have changed my life so much, because it was the very magnitude of that horror that created the potential for change.

Walking the ordeal path means recognizing value in the suffering we cannot avoid in life. That value is not derived from the good that comes later, but exists within the suffering itself. If life were a book, then society tells us to skip over or skim through the chapters on pain and suffering, and to focus on the chapters about joy and pleasure. The ordeal path reminds us that the chapters about joy and pleasure are informed by the chapters on pain and suffering, and the book as a whole has greater meaning if you read the whole thing.

We often do not get to choose what suffering we must endure in life, but we can choose to engage with that suffering as seekers. To do so means accepting that even when we can't imagine what good could possibly come of a thing, there is some good that can come of it, and this is not the same as saying that the thing itself was good. In that moment, when everything is terrible and we can't imagine how this could possibly help us, we must embrace the uncertainty of ordeal, feel the full force of our agony, and seek what we can learn about ourselves in our darkest moments.

Looking back now on my divorce, I evaluate that experience very differently. It was not the good life I made for myself by leaving that shows the value of the experience, but rather my willingness to suffer for the person I wanted to be. I am secure in my identity because I know how terrible it is to hide myself, and because choosing to live authentically was one of the most painful decisions I've ever made. Ignoring that pain would devalue the entire experience. If the choice to leave had been easy, it would not have pushed me to grow so much. To this day, people remark how I came back from Europe a different person. They are right.

There is no misery benchmark one must meet in order to walk the ordeal path. The point is not how much something hurts, but what you can learn from the hurt. Furthermore, suffering is both individual and relative to each person's life experience.

Before my divorce, my most emotionally agonizing experience was a specific breakup. Looking back on that relationship more than a decade and a half later, I'm almost embarrassed by the thoughts, values, and actions of my former self. It's easy to minimize that experience now that I've lived through so much worse, and now that my priorities have changed such that what was important to me then is trivial now. Nevertheless, doing so would be a discredit not only to my own life journey, but also to everyone else who suffers differently than I do. I am a different person now precisely because of how that breakup changed me. I questioned my values in its aftermath, and reshaped myself into a healthier person thanks to what I learned through that loss. I was able to endure worse later in life precisely because of the strength I gained back then.

If even my own measure of suffering changes during my life, then of course other people with completely different lives will experience pain differently from me. There is no objective measure for suffering, because suffering is not an objective thing. Walking the ordeal path means resisting the impulse to compare your suffering to that of others. It doesn't matter if it could be worse, or if it's so much more terrible. What matters is how it feels to you, and whether you choose to embrace that feeling as an opportunity for personal growth.

That choice can only be made by the individual suffering. None of us are ever qualified to judge for another whether or not some experience of theirs ought to be engaged with as an ordeal. You may make that decision for your own life, but no one else may make it for you. Pressuring someone to walk the ordeal path when that is not their choice undermines their agency. That agency is critical for ordeal work, so your pressure will not at all help, only hinder.

This is particularly important for individuals living with chronic illness or disabilities. Society is quick to tell people with these types of experiences how they should heal, how they should struggle, how they should be helped, how they should inspire others, how they should inspire themselves, how they should live … and yet we so rarely listen to what they want for themselves. Telling a person who is blind, for example, that they should embrace their blindness as an ordeal not only adds to the onslaught against their agency, it also casts judgment upon their blindness, which may not at all be resonant with their experience of it. Perhaps they do not feel their blindness is a source of suffering, and your assumption that it would be is simply hurtful. We should never make these types of valuations for other people. Only an individual may determine what is suffering for them.

If you decide that your chronic illness or disability is something you want to engage with as an ordeal, then remember that choosing to do so doesn't mean you think your illness or disability is a good thing. It means validating how hard it is to live with and deriving personal power from your suffering. It means recognizing that something can still be terrible, even when it makes you a better person, because it's not really that thing that made you better, but *you*—how *you* learned from your suffering, and what *you* did with what you learned. The thing that caused your suffering will always be terrible, and because it is terrible, it can show you how you are powerful.

Chapter 28: Cultivating Resilience

Resilience is relevant to all types of ordeal work. Recognizing and utilizing internal and external resilience factors will be helpful to a seeker regardless of what type of ordeal they face, so the concepts put forth in the chapters on Safer Seeking and The Art of Becoming apply to the ordeal path as well as to ordeal ritual. In ritual, however, facilitators can attempt to aid the seeker by highlighting areas where the seeker is most supported, and providing extra support when it is most needed. When we are both seeker and facilitator for our own life's ordeals, we must do this work for ourselves.

This process begins with recognizing systemic privilege and oppression. Dismantling oppression is important work that is beyond the scope of this book. Ordeal is necessarily self-centered, so our focus is limited to individual internal experience. The ways in which an individual lacks privilege make it harder for that person to constructively integrate painful life experiences. Positive change through suffering is certainly possible, but it will just as certainly be harder when one's resources are sapped by coping with their disadvantages.

When I say "harder" here, I do not mean harder for one individual than for another. Once again, comparisons between people are not useful for our purposes in this book. It is harder for a disadvantaged person to process a life-ordeal than it would be *for that same person* if they were not disadvantaged. This may seem obvious, but it is important to recognize, both so that we can exercise some compassion for ourselves when we walk a difficult path, and so that we may validate our own experience of life by recognizing its challenges.

Validation boosts resilience, so finding strength in unfair circumstances begins with acknowledging just how difficult systemic oppression is. If you feel that your path is made more challenging or exhausting by the fact that you are, for example, poor, transgender, neurodivergent, have a disability, or are a person of color … that's because it is. This path does not require you to change how society treats you; all it requires is recognition of your struggle. In *Chapter 30: Witnessing Change*, we will examine how to find external validation. For the moment, know that you can also validate yourself.

Recognizing and validating your own experience is so crucial because the process of cultivating resilience begins with allowing yourself to feel whatever and however you feel. Embrace your emotions and allow them to be what they are. Give yourself time to grieve, to cry, to scream, to curl up alone in your room, or to do whatever else is, by your own definition and determination, a satisfying expression of your feelings. You get to decide how long to spend in this first stage of validation and expression. Give your feelings the time that they need, and when you are ready, move on.

The next step is to make a conscious choice to treat your experience as an ordeal. Agency is critical to resilience, and in ordeal ritual we reinforce agency through consent: the seeker chooses to proceed with the ritual, and is able to end it at any time. In life we usually can't control the event that is the source of our suffering, so instead we affirm our agency by choosing whether or not to engage with that event as an ordeal experience. While this book, being all about ordeal, certainly has a bias in that direction, this choice is deeply personal, and must be made without any preconception of what one *should* do. Ritualizing an experience is not the only way to learn and grow through pain, and making a choice could not support agency if only one outcome were acceptable.

Once you have decided to proceed with ordeal work, you must seek insight in your suffering. What is beyond your control? What is within your control? What are you willing to change, and what must remain in order for you to be true to who you are? How will you adapt to what life has delivered? Choosing how to act will be difficult, but in the act of choosing you will learn about who you are.

Change is often overwhelming, and we can become stuck in suffering when we don't know how to follow through with the changes we've chosen for ourselves. Following the breakup I mentioned in the last chapter, I decided that I never again wanted a relationship to define my life's worth, so I needed to fundamentally transform my priorities, figure out what I lived for, and decide what I wanted to do with my life. This change certainly did not happen overnight. The first step was to find a therapist and seek help. In the beginning I was too unwell to manage anything more than that, so I worked on an intricate art project while I waited for my first appointment, thus keeping my mind occupied and my emotions distracted.

Small practical steps are key to success. Had I expected myself to immediately feel independently valuable, I would have wound up further depressed by a failure to accomplish my goal. I didn't know how to go about changing the values written into me in my upbringing, or even how much there was to untangle, or how many aspects of my life it would touch. I just knew that I needed to change, and wanted somewhere to start. Seeing a therapist was a concrete goal, and following through with that plan gave me a sense of accomplishment. I wasn't yet where I wanted to be, but I was working on it. That alone was progress worth being proud of.

As you decide what steps to take in response to your ordeal experience, consider actions that are practical, specific, and attainable. Seeing a therapist was practical for me because I lived in an urban area where finding an appropriate therapist was relatively easy, and I had excellent health insurance at the time. Seeing a therapist was a specific action, attainable through even a single visit. If my first therapist ended up being a poor fit for me, I could continue searching for one I worked well with, but would still have fulfilled my first goal of seeing a therapist at all. In that early stage I held no qualifications for success involving results from therapy; the goal was itself just getting therapy at all.

As my process continued, I could add more specific and attainable goals that built upon prior successes. Having found a therapist I liked, my goal was then to go to therapy once a week. As therapy began to help me understand myself better, I was able to set and accomplish practical goals in other areas of my life. My thought process was not so declarative at the time; I did not go through a formal process of setting goals and marking them off a list, and did not explicitly understand what made these smaller goals more successful. That first step of seeing a therapist was just all I felt I could manage at the time, and from there conversations with my therapist helped me find reasonable steps towards becoming the person I wanted to be.

Today my process often *is* so declarative, but only when that level of structure is helpful. Sometimes carefully planning our steps gives us a concrete way to measure progress. At other times all we can do is just take things one day at a time, and progress is measured in another day done. The point is to derive satisfaction from small victories and gradual progress, whatever form that might take.

Remember that having a new goal doesn't erase the fact that you accomplished the one that came before. If we don't take time to appreciate what we've done, we end up feeling like we never accomplish anything. Remember also that every day won't be a good day, and that's ok. All of us will stumble now and then, and a little backtracking doesn't undo the entirety of your progress.

Ordeal itself offers resilience just by choosing to walk the path at all. The ordeal path says that if you look in the mirror and don't like who you see, that's OK, because you can change. You're still doing it "right" because you looked in the mirror at all. The ordeal path insists that we must all constantly change, because growth is change, so if you're examining yourself well enough to see where change is needed, then you are making progress and deserve to be proud of your work.

Chapter 29: Avoiding Expectation

Expectation might seem easier to avoid on the ordeal path, since one never knows what life will bring next. Keep in mind, however, that it is expectation regarding outcome of which we must be wary, and this is just as true in life's ordeals as it is in ordeal ritual. Our intent on the ordeal path is to cultivate personal power through the pain we must endure. If we go into that suffering with an idea of what that power will be, or who we will become on the other side, that becomes the type of expectation that will hinder our growth.

When life demands that we struggle, we might feel tempted to rationalize our experience, focusing on what we can gain on the other side of that struggle. For example, during the process of my divorce, at times I felt tempted to ignore all the ways in which I hurt, and everything I had to leave behind, instead focusing on how much better my life would be when everything was over and done. That might have helped me get through everything, but I wouldn't have learned as much about myself had I not acknowledged my pain enough to examine why it hurt, and what it said about me that I was willing to leave even though it hurt as much as it did. I'm not a better person because I got a divorce. I'm a better person because I treated my divorce like a book about my deeper self, and dared to read what it said about me.

Ordeal's power is in suffering itself. Holding an intent that we will learn *something* in suffering certainly helps our resilience, but an expectation of *what* we will learn can blind us to other potential insights. The uncertainty that transforms suffering into an ordeal comes from not knowing how an experience will transform you, and embracing the suffering anyway in order to learn its lesson.

As seekers on the ordeal path we must hold in our minds a balance between our goal of empowerment and the necessity of suffering. Focusing exclusively on the positive outcome we hope for not only draws our attention away from exactly what we are supposed to be learning from, but also leads to the "silver lining" mentality that ultimately minimizes, marginalizes, or outright ignores the significance of our experiences. The ordeal path teaches us the value of being present in the moment, fully immersed in experiencing what we are living. How you hold your intent must not detract from holistic engagement.

As you travel your path, remember that growth and pain are not mutually exclusive. Seek your power, let that intent carry you through darkness, and also welcome that darkness as the only place where you will be able find what you are hiding from yourself. To know more, you must venture into the unknown.

Chapter 30: Witnessing Change

Suffering is deeply personal, and sometimes we want or even need to bear it alone. When my father died, I never wanted to cry in front of anyone else, not even my family. His loss was a private experience for me, and while I sometimes wonder if my aunts and uncles know how keenly I mourn him, I still need hold that sorrow on my own. Witnessing my own grief was critical to my ordeal process.

Normally I am the type to keep a journal, self-witnessing my thoughts and feelings on hand-written pages. This was a major part of how I processed my divorce, and it is how I have worked through a great many other issues throughout my life. My father's death, however, was too much to write about. The most I could manage in the first year was a sentence or two just recording the fact that he was dead. Instead, witnessing myself came in the form of allowing myself time to grieve. I needed time away from the world, and took it without feeling guilty or ashamed. While I do regret the computer gaming habits of some other phases of my life, disappearing into another world during those weeks after my father had died were needed. Taking that time with compassion for myself became a way of witnessing my own hurt. I validated the intensity of the experience by recognizing and responding to my needs for recovery.

When life delivers an ordeal you need to face alone, give yourself time and space to feel and express your emotions. If something that has always helped you before suddenly doesn't work, that's OK. Every situation is different, and our needs change over time. Consider modifying a coping strategy that was successful in the past. For example, if you typically benefit from journaling but find yourself unable to sit still with a notebook and pen, try typing your entry instead of hand-writing it, or make an audio recording of your reflections on your experience. Keep in mind that the point is not to share your writings or recordings, but to give your thoughts and feelings an arena for expression. If modifications don't work, that's OK too. Sometimes what you need is completely different, and discovering that need might be part of the ordeal process.

Having even a single person you can talk to about what you're going through can sometimes make the difference between an impossible obstacle and a navigable ordeal. When I struggle with family or childhood issues, I know that I can always talk to my sister when I need to be witnessed. If I'm facing challenges in other areas of my life, my domestic partner will hold space for me to express my feelings when that is what I need. Think about the people close to you, and consider who might be able to listen and witness your journey on the ordeal path. Not every individual will be right for every type of ordeal, and that's OK. The point is not for them to give advice or tell you how to respond, but just to hear you out and validate your experience.

Witnessing someone's ordeal, especially when you're the only person to do so, can be difficult. Holding space can be emotionally exhausting even when the issue at hand is not an ordeal. Knowing that this is a heavy request can make us reluctant to ask for it, and the solution to that reluctance rests in *how* we ask. When you want someone to witness your ordeal path experience, start with letting them know that you want to talk about a heavy subject, and ask if that's all right. Give the person an opportunity to say whether or not they have the emotional resources to handle something intense in that moment. If they can't, accept their answer and respect their limits. Asking on more general terms first gives the person an opportunity to gracefully decline if they're not up for emotional intensity, and accepting a "no" will also be easier for you if you haven't yet told them much about what you're going through. If the person is willing to hear more, then you can clarify what that subject is, and make sure they're comfortable holding space for that particular topic. Acknowledge the importance of what you're asking for, and thank the person for the effort they will expend in holding space for you. Asking permission and showing appreciation for their emotional labor will help you feel more comfortable expressing yourself to them, will help them feel valued, and, most importantly, creates informed consent for everyone.

When we do want other people to witness our journey, a community that will support us on the ordeal path is invaluable. Remember to keep a broad definition of community as you seek people who might offer validation: family, chosen family, friends, partners, and religious groups are just a few examples of communities that might be willing and able to witness you. While it might help to be able to use the ordeal vocabulary presented in this book, keep in mind that my terminology is not required for a constructive experience. You can talk to people about seeking and suffering if you wish, or you can leave those terms aside entirely and simply relay your experience. Share whatever and however you feel comfortable.

Even when you can't specifically speak with a community about your ordeal experience, sometimes being validated in other ways still helps build resilience overall. Attending conventions with rich spiritual community is a deeply rejuvenating experience for me. No matter what else I might be going through in my life, spending time with other people who share an understanding of spirituality and energy work leaves me feeling ready and able to tackle whatever comes next. Being seen, acknowledged, understood, accepted, and appreciated builds a strength that is nonspecific. The next trial I face could have nothing to do with spirituality, and I will still be better able to face it. If you don't have a community with which you can openly discuss ordeal, keep in mind that time spent with any type of affirming community can still help your overall process.

Seeking community on the internet can produce very mixed results. Sometimes just knowing that you are not alone in your experience is invaluable, while other times knowing that the only people you can talk to are physically far away is just more isolating. The general atmosphere of the group also makes a difference in whether or not it will help you. At my therapist's suggestion, I joined an online chronic pain forum in hopes of finding a peer group that could validate my experience of dealing with spine problems. Ultimately, however, I found the group to be tremendously depressing. My therapist wasn't wrong in urging me to seek community; rather, the group I joined simply didn't have an atmosphere of mutual support.

Validation isn't something that just automatically happens when people assemble. The individuals in a community must choose to support one another by acknowledging each other's experiences. When you are trying to decide whether or not an online or in-person group is likely to help your process, pay attention to how its members interact with one another. Recognition, compassion, and respect are essential for a positive support structure.

In the end, everything comes back to you. If other people just don't understand what you're going through, that's all right. They don't have to. It is *your* spirit you've been suffering for, not theirs. Even when you've had an army of friends and family supporting you, ultimately it is your own recognition of self that matters most. What did you find in darkness? Who were you, and who have you become?

Ultimate validation comes at the end of ordeal, when you reap the fruits of your anguish by claiming your identity and living it. Journey into suffering to experience the spirit who you are. Emerge as a honed expression of yourself.

Epilogue: The Fool's Journey

Finishing this book is almost as terrifying as writing it was. When I began learning about ritual ordeal, the popular opinion at the time was that ordeal work is so dangerous that information about it should not be publicly available. My response to this is that people will continue to do ordeal work whether I write about it or not. I want to help the people who choose that work make as informed a choice as possible about how they engage with it.

Even so, I have at times struggled to put words to the page. Who am I to write these things? I am not a trained psychologist or therapist, but I am writing about the inner workings of mind and heart. Will people be helped or harmed by the words here? I think I have a solid understanding of what I'm doing and how it works, but what if I'm wrong? I could not go around preaching the concepts of ordeal without being willing to explore these shadows of doubt within myself.

Those Tarot cards I studied as a teenager make a lot more sense now. Tarot is made up of "Major Arcana" and "Minor Arcana" cards. The Minor Arcana consists of four suits, with a clear connection to playing cards. The Major Arcana consists of 22 unique cards, and there are several interpretations of their significance. One of those interpretations is known as "The Fool's Journey".

All of the Major Arcana are numbered, starting with the Magician at number 1, up through the World at number 21. The Fool's number is 0. This causes some to believe the card belongs at the very beginning of the major arcana, the number 0 representing a fresh start. Other interpretations suggest that the Fool is both the end and the beginning, being the step at which the cycle of the Major Arcana is renewed.

The concept of the Fool's Journey suggests that the Fool exists as a traveler throughout the entirety of the Major Arcana, experiencing each of the cards as a journey through life. The Fool is the archetypical seeker, ignorant and innocent, who must take a risk in order to learn, who will inevitably be hurt, and who, through hurt, will grow in joy, in love, and in personal power.

The Fool's Journey is among those interpretations that places the Fool card at both the beginning and the end of the Major Arcana. One journey leads to another, and our cycles of transformation never end. How, then, does the World, a card representing fulfillment and completion, become the Fool all over again? One could argue that the World becomes the Fool through arrogance: when we think we know everything, we have forgotten the most important lesson of all, that none of us will ever know everything. One could also argue that the World becomes the Fool when wisdom shows us what we still have to learn.

So here I am, finally at the end of this book, typing the last few words, wondering if I was right to do so, and I ask myself: am I so arrogant that I don't even know how much of a novice I am? Or have I come full circle to begin a new cycle with all the wisdom I gained the last time around? The answer is probably a little of both.

Thank you for joining me on this journey. Wherever your path goes from here, take care as you travel, and remember: be all that you are, and be only what you are.

Appendix: Suggested Resources

Books:

- *Sacred Pain: Hurting the Body for the Sake of the Soul* by Ariel Glucklich. Oxford University Press, Inc., 2001
- *The Body Keeps the Score: Brain, Mind, and Body in the Healing of Trauma* by Bessel van der Kolk, M.D. Penguin Books, 2014
- *Trauma and Memory: Brain and Body in a Search for the Living Past: A Practical Guide for Understanding and Working with Traumatic Memory* by Peter A. Levine PhD. North Atlantic Books, 2015
- *Dark Moon Rising: Pagan BDSM and the Ordeal Path* by Raven Kaldera. Asphodel Press, 2006
- *Sacred Kink: The Eightfold Paths of BDSM and Beyond* by Lee Harrington. Mystic Productions Press, 2016
- *Wightridden: Paths of Northern-Tradition Shamanism* by Raven Kaldera. Asphodel Press, 2007
- *Spirit + Flesh* by Fakir Musafar. Arena Editions, 2015
- *Modern Primitives: Tattoo, Piercing, Scarification- An Investigation of Contemporary Adornment & Ritual* edited by V. Vale and Andrea Juno. Re/search, 1989
- *Pagan Consent Culture: Building Communities of Empathy & Autonomy* edited by Christine Hoff Kraemer. Asphodel Press, 2016
- *Leatherfolk: Radical Sex, People, Politics, and Practice* by Mark Thompson. Daedalus Publishing, 2004

Other Resources:

- National Coalition for Sexual Freedom: https://www.ncsfreedom.org/

NCSF Mission Statement:

The NCSF is committed to creating a political, legal and social environment in the US that advances equal rights for consenting adults who engage in alternative sexual and relationship expressions. The NCSF aims to advance the rights of, and advocate for consenting adults in the BDSM-

Leather-Fetish, Swing, and Polyamory Communities. We pursue our vision through direct services, education, advocacy, and outreach, in conjunction with our partners, to directly benefit these communities.

Of particular relevance to this book is the NCSF's Kink Aware Professionals directory, a database that includes various types of mental health professionals who might be open to talking about ordeal with their clients. This database is a useful tool for finding professional help, but it cannot guarantee a good fit between client and therapist. It is offered as a helpful starting point in a longer search process.

- ❖ Psychology Today's database of gay therapists: https://www.psychologytoday.com/us/therapists/gay

Psychology Today offers an online database of therapists, and through this link that database is automatically filtered to include only those professionals who support gay clients. Due to the high amount of crossover between the LGBTQIA+ and kinky communities, these professionals are more likely to be kink-aware, and thus may be open to discussing ordeal with their clients. This database is a useful tool for finding professional help, but it cannot guarantee a good fit between client and therapist. It is offered as a helpful starting point in a longer search process.

www.ingramcontent.com/pod-product-compliance
Lightning Source LLC
Chambersburg PA
CBHW031145160426
43193CB00008B/260